Cookir
for
Slimmers

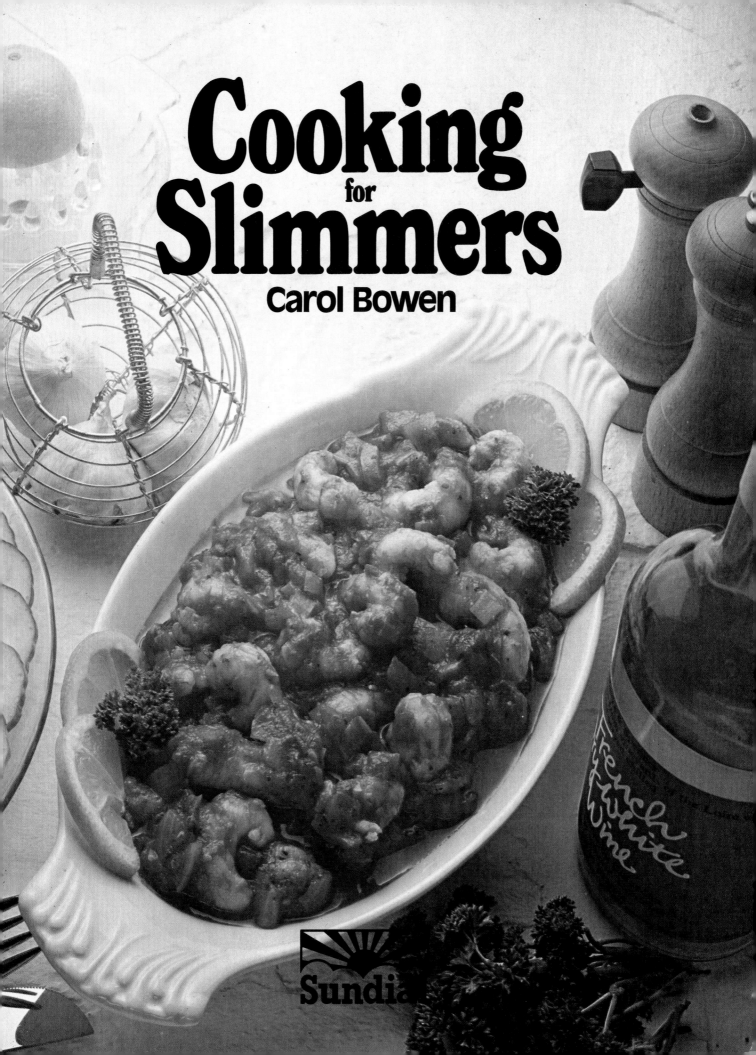

Cooking
for
Slimmers
Carol Bowen

Sundial

Contents

First published in 1977 by Sundial Books Limited
59 Grosvenor Street, London W1

Fifth impression, 1979

© 1977 Hennerwood Publications Limited
ISBN 0 904230 47 3

Printed in England by Severn Valley Press Limited

Introduction

If you are reading this book you probably want to slim. Whether for health or social reasons the way to do it is the same—you must eat less. A sad fact, stated many times, but simple to understand if you think about it.

Just like a car, the human body needs fuel—food and drink. Once your body has enough fuel it will convert any surplus into a storage fuel—fat. The only time when the stored fuel will be used is when the fuel supply is inadequate. So cutting down on the amount of food and drink you consume is the only way of getting rid of fat, by forcing your body to use it up.

There are two basic ways of eating less: calorie-cutting and carbohydrate-cutting. This book follows the former method because it is recognisably a much more flexible way of dieting. It fits in with the family routine, social arrangements and your own whims and fancies.

Calorie-cutting simply means keeping a check on the calorie values of the food you eat, and the aim should be to take in fewer calories than you expend. The amount of weight you lose and the rate at which it goes will depend upon how much you cut that input.

But what is a calorie?

A calorie is the unit we use to measure energy value in foods, and the total energy value of any food or drink, measured in calories, depends upon the nutrients it contains. We all need a certain balance of these nutrients—proteins, fats, carbohydrates, minerals and vitamins for our physical and mental well-being. So the diet and dishes you choose to make up your calorie

allowance must be well-balanced enough to meet the body's day-to-day needs, while at the same time being tasty and appetising enough to satisfy you. The metric equivalent of the calorie is the kilojoule (kJ).

Choice of calorie allowance is very much a personal matter. As a guideline remember that you need a calorie deficit of 3,500 calories (15,000 kJ) to lose one pound ($\frac{1}{2}$ kg) in weight. So if on average you are using up 2,000 calories (8,500 kJ) a day, and you are eating and drinking an average of 1,500 calories (6,500 kJ) a day, your daily calorie (kJ) deficit will be 500 calories (2,000 kJ), and you should lose a pound a week. (In fact during the first week of dieting you will lose more, because you are losing extra water from your body as well as fat.)

By controlling this deficit you can choose how quickly you lose your weight. However it is better to be sensible about this and to choose a realistic calorie allowance, one that you can stick to comfortably and so will not give up too easily.

As a simple general guide set your intake of calories at 1,500 (6,500 kJ) or 1,000 calories (4,000 kJ) per day, according to whether you have under or over 2 stones (12·7 kg) to lose respectively.

Living with your diet

Having decided upon your calorie allowance per day, you will need to keep a check on the calorie values of the foods you eat. For convenience the basic ones have been listed at the back of this book. You will soon become familiar with the amount and calorie values of foods.

But setting your calorie allowance at a certain figure each day does not mean that you have to stick strictly to this limit. It is far better to plan

on a weekly basis and spread your calorie allowance over the days. For example, most of us tend to eat more at the weekend, so it may be wise to save up some of that mid-week allowance to indulge in this feasting. In the same way, when you eat too much one day, perhaps for social reasons, you can make up for it next day by having fewer calories.

The way in which you spread your calorie allowance throughout the day is again a personal one. It will depend on whether you have your main meal at lunch time or in the evening. But tests have shown that taking your food in several small snacks or meals rather than one large and heavy meal can be the most satisfying way to lose weight.

Being on a diet need not be dreary, as I hope this book will show you. It is possible to provide interesting and nourishing meals with low-calorie ingredients. Lean meat, fish, offal, poultry, fresh fruit, green vegetables, eggs and certain cheeses are all suitable foods, as well as the ever-increasing number of low-calorie diet extras making their way into the shops.

The intake of calories can be reduced not only by eating the right food but also by ensuring that cooking methods do not make food more fattening. Bake, grill, steam and braise food rather than fry or roast it with extra fat. Or 'fry' in a non-stick pan with just a smear of butter or oil.

Slimming aids

Everyone who has grimly soldiered on through a slimming diet must have at some time prayed for a miracle food, injection or pill that could literally melt away the fat. Scientists have come up with a few answers, namely substitute foods, diet extras, bread, sugar and drink replacements.

Substitute foods basically amount to complete milk meals that have all the nutrients you require for a healthy slimming diet. Unfortunately they prove to be a very boring way to lose weight if taken alone, but they can play a useful role as part of an ordinary slimming diet. The latest versions of these foods include diet biscuits (usually taken with milk), diet soups and ready-prepared meals.

Diet foods are no substitute for proper eating habits. It is far better to train your appetite to accept less food and low-calorie eating. Also they rarely fit in with normal family meal routines and are an expensive way of slimming.

As well as products intended to replace whole meals, there is a variety of diet extras that are intended to replace individual items of the diet. These include low-calorie cordials, low-calorie breakfast cereals, jams and spreads

and low-calorie minerals. They are a welcome extra to any slimmer's diet – but will help you to lose weight only as part of a calorie-controlled diet.

Perhaps the most successful diet food replacements are starch-reduced bread and crispbreads, low-calorie spreads and artificial sweeteners in tablet and liquid forms (most powders contain some calories). Perhaps this is because they represent such basic foods in our diets. There seems to be no reason why you should not take full advantage of them in your diet, and indeed many of the recipes in this book use them in some form or other to cut the calories in favourite dishes. Do not become confused with special diabetic products readily found on chemists' shelves as these are specially prepared for diabetes patients and will not help you lose weight.

Checking your progress

One of the best ways to spur yourself on when you are trying to lose weight is to keep a record of your progress. A graph pinned to the wall can give you encouragement just when you are beginning to falter. First check your ideal weight on the table opposite. Decide when, where and how you are going to weigh yourself (your lightest time will be first thing in the morning), then weigh yourself three times a week and plot a record of your weight as you progress through your diet. It will also give you a fair indication of when you will reach your ideal weight.

Tips

Making the decision to go on a diet can be very simple. Sticking to your diet, however, can be a very different affair. If you suffer from hunger pangs in the early stages of your diet don't make a rush for the biscuit tin but nibble at carrot, celery and other vegetable sticks. Fill yourself up with a hot cup of black coffee, lemon tea or beef extract drink. Or spoil yourself with a low-calorie mineral cheerfully chinking with ice and lemon.

Even the best well-balanced diet can sometimes lead to constipation. Plenty of fresh fruit, vegetables and salad in your diet can help to correct this. Also if your calorie allowance runs to it eat brown and wholemeal bread. Natural unprocessed bran is also helpful. Try two teaspoons three times a day with your meals, and also drink plenty of low-calorie fluids.
★ Remember, before starting any calorie-controlled diet, to check with your doctor that there are no reasons why you should not do so.
All spoon measurements are level.
All recipes serve four unless otherwise stated.

Table of desirable weights

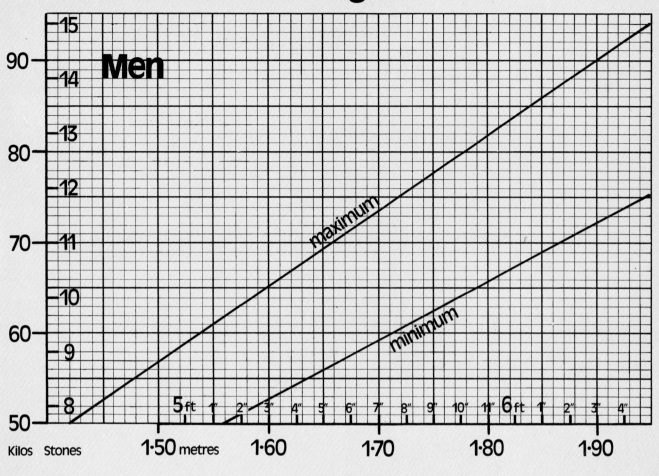

Men

maximum

minimum

15					
90	14				
	13				
80	12				
70	11				
	10				
60	9				
	8				
50					

Kilos Stones

5ft 1" 2" 3" 4" 5" 6" 7" 8" 9" 10" 11" 6ft 1" 2" 3" 4"

1·50 metres   1·60   1·70   1·80   1·90

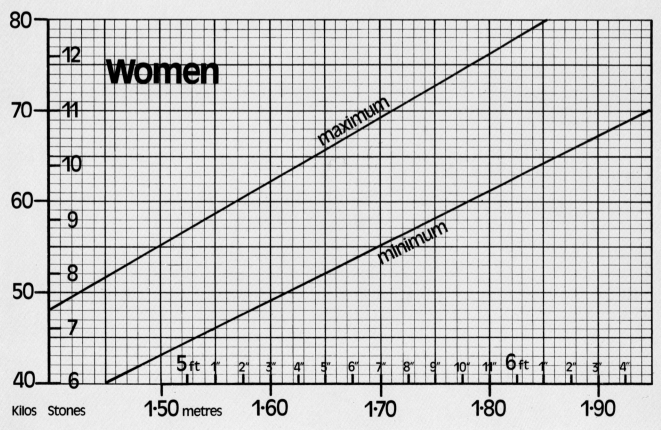

Women

maximum

minimum

80					
	12				
70	11				
	10				
60	9				
	8				
50	7				
40	6				

Kilos Stones

5ft 1" 2" 3" 4" 5" 6" 7" 8" 9" 10" 11" 6ft 1" 2" 3" 4"

1·50 metres   1·60   1·70   1·80   1·90

A tasty, well-blended soup can be the basis for many a slimmer's meal, without running the risk of becoming monotonous. Use soups adventurously, and you will rarely falter from your diet.

Hot or cold, thick or thin, the vital ingredient for a good soup is a well-prepared stock. Use the carcass of a chicken as the basis for a white stock, marrow or veal bones for a meaty brown or beef stock, and fish heads and bones for a fish stock. Simmer with a few chopped vegetables and a bouquet garni for about 3–4 hours. Then, most important for slimmers, skim off the fat before use. The easiest way to do this is to put the stock in a refrigerator and, when cool, lift the fat from the surface of the stock as a solid cake.

Stock cubes and concentrates can also be used as convenient, instant alternatives to home-made stock. But care must be taken when seasoning since they already contain a sizeable proportion of salt in them. An average stock cube contains about 16 calories. Use the stock to make low-calorie consommés, filling and satisfying vegetable soups and broths, or, as the basis for a more substantial main meal, meaty soups. Top with low-calorie garnishes, such as yogurt, low-calorie bread croûtons or strips of vegetable.

Gazpacho

Metric

½ kg ripe juicy tomatoes, skinned
1 large onion, peeled
1 small green pepper, deseeded and chopped
1 clove garlic, skinned and finely chopped
1 × 15 ml spoon wine vinegar
1 × 15 ml spoon olive oil
1–2 × 15 ml spoons lemon juice
150 ml tomato juice
Salt and freshly ground black pepper

To finish:
½ cucumber, peeled and diced
Croûtons made from low-calorie bread, toasted

Imperial

1 lb ripe juicy tomatoes, skinned
1 large onion, peeled
1 small green pepper, deseeded and chopped
1 clove garlic, skinned and finely chopped
1 tablespoon wine vinegar
1 tablespoon olive oil
1–2 tablespoons lemon juice
¼ pint tomato juice
Salt and freshly ground black pepper

To finish:
½ cucumber, peeled and diced
Croûtons made from low-calorie bread, toasted

Purée the tomatoes, chopped onion, green pepper, garlic, vinegar and olive oil in a blender, or push through a fine sieve. Turn into a basin, add the lemon juice and tomato juice, season to taste and chill thoroughly in the refrigerator. Serve sprinkled with the diced cucumber and croûtons.
Calories per portion: 80 300 kJ (excluding croûtons)

Gardener's broth; Minestrone; Fish chowder

Fish chowder

Metric

2 rashers lean bacon,
derinded and chopped
1 onion, peeled and sliced
½ kg fresh haddock, cooked
and flaked
396 g can tomatoes
2 potatoes, peeled and diced
300 ml fish stock
Salt and freshly ground
black pepper
Bay leaf
2 cloves
150 ml skimmed milk

To finish:
1 × 15 ml spoon finely
chopped parsley

Imperial

2 rashers lean bacon,
derinded and chopped
1 onion, peeled and sliced
1 lb fresh haddock, cooked
and flaked
14 oz can tomatoes
2 potatoes, peeled and diced
½ pint fish stock
Salt and freshly ground
black pepper
Bay leaf
2 cloves
¼ pint skimmed milk

To finish:
1 tablespoon finely
chopped parsley

Cooking Time: 40 minutes

Fry the bacon until the fat runs. Add the onion and sauté until clear—about 5 minutes. Add the fish, tomatoes and potatoes, with the stock and seasonings. Simmer gently for about ½ hour. Add the milk and remove the bay leaf and cloves. Reheat gently. Serve piping hot sprinkled with the chopped parsley.

Calories per portion: 225 900 kJ

Minestrone

Metric

75 g haricot beans
900 ml white stock
1 onion, peeled and finely chopped
1 × 15 ml spoon olive oil
1 clove garlic, crushed
25 g lean bacon, diced
Salt and freshly ground black pepper
2 × 15 ml spoons finely chopped celery
225 g tomatoes, peeled and deseeded
1 large carrot, diced
225 g cabbage, finely shredded
50 g macaroni

To finish:
25 g Parmesan cheese, finely grated
1 × 15 ml spoon finely chopped parsley

Imperial

3 oz haricot beans
1½ pints white stock
1 onion, peeled and finely chopped
1 tablespoon olive oil
1 clove garlic, crushed
1 oz lean bacon, diced
Salt and freshly ground black pepper
2 tablespoons finely chopped celery
8 oz tomatoes, peeled and deseeded
1 large carrot, diced
8 oz cabbage, finely shredded
2 oz macaroni

To finish:
1 oz Parmesan cheese, finely grated
1 tablespoon finely chopped parsley

Cooking Time: 2 hours

Soak the haricot beans overnight in the stock. Heat the oil and toss the onion in it, with the garlic and bacon. Add to the haricot beans, season to taste and simmer gently for about 1½ hours. Add all remaining vegetables except the cabbage and cook for a further 20 minutes, adding a little more stock if needed. Add the cabbage and macaroni and cook until both are just tender. Adjust seasoning. Serve topped with the Parmesan and garnished with chopped parsley.
Calories per portion: 224 900 kJ

Gardener's broth

Metric

1 rasher lean bacon
25 g butter
2–3 small onions, peeled and sliced
2–3 small carrots, scrubbed and sliced
Small piece of turnip
1 l stock or water
2 tomatoes, peeled and sliced
2–3 runner beans, topped and tailed
Few leaves young cabbage
Salt and freshly ground black pepper
Pinch mixed herbs
25 g short-cut macaroni

To finish:
Grated cheese
1 × 15 ml spoon finely chopped parsley

Imperial

1 rasher lean bacon
1 oz butter
2–3 small onions, peeled and sliced
2–3 small carrots, scrubbed and sliced
Small piece of turnip
1¾ pints stock or water
2 tomatoes, peeled and sliced
2–3 runner beans, topped and tailed
Few leaves young cabbage
Salt and freshly ground black pepper
Pinch mixed herbs
1 oz short-cut macaroni

To finish:
Grated cheese
1 tablespoon finely chopped parsley

Cooking Time: 1 hour

Rind and dice the bacon, put in a pan with the butter and onions and sauté until soft. Add the carrot and turnip and cook for a further 5 minutes. Pour in the stock or water and bring to the boil. Add the rest of the vegetables, seasoning and herbs, then cover and simmer for ¾ hour. Add the macaroni and simmer for a further 15 minutes. Serve piping hot sprinkled with grated cheese and chopped parsley.
Calories per portion: 155 650 kJ

Pot-au-feu

Pot-au-feu

Metric

1 l well-flavoured
stock
225 g chuck steak, cut into
cubes
4 carrots, scrubbed and
diced
2 bay leaves
Rosemary sprig
2 × 15 ml spoons long-
grain rice
3 leeks, washed and sliced
Small cauliflower, washed
and broken into florets
100 g peas
2 tomatoes, skinned and
diced
Salt and freshly ground
black pepper
Pinch of cayenne pepper

Imperial

1¾ pints well-flavoured
stock
8 oz chuck steak, cut into
cubes
4 carrots, scrubbed and
diced
2 bay leaves
Rosemary sprig
2 tablespoons long-grain
rice
3 leeks, washed and sliced
Small cauliflower, washed
and broken into florets
4 oz peas
2 tomatoes, skinned and
diced
Salt and freshly ground
black pepper
Pinch of cayenne pepper

Cooking Time: 2 hours

Put the stock into a large saucepan. Add the steak and carrots with the bay leaves and rosemary. Bring to the boil and simmer gently for 1–1½ hours. Add the rice, leeks, cauliflower and peas and simmer for a further 15–20 minutes. Remove the bay leaves and rosemary and add the tomatoes and seasonings to taste. Cook for a further 5 minutes. Serve piping hot.
Calories per portion: 175 700 kJ

Borsch

Borsch

Metric	Imperial
10 g beef dripping	*¼ oz beef dripping*
1 large raw beetroot, peeled and grated	*1 large raw beetroot, peeled and grated*
1 carrot, scrubbed and grated	*1 carrot, scrubbed and grated*
1 onion, peeled and finely chopped	*1 onion, peeled and finely chopped*
350 g red cabbage, finely grated	*12 oz red cabbage, finely grated*
2 tomatoes, peeled and chopped	*2 tomatoes, peeled and chopped*
1 l white stock	*1¾ pints white stock*
Salt and freshly ground black pepper	*Salt and freshly ground black pepper*
2 bay leaves	*2 bay leaves*
Pinch of mixed herbs	*Pinch of mixed herbs*

To finish:
Natural yogurt
1 × 15 ml spoon finely chopped parsley

To finish:
Natural yogurt
1 tablespoon finely chopped parsley

Cooking Time: 2 hours

Melt the dripping in a large heavy-based pan and fry the grated beetroot lightly for 5 minutes. Add the remaining vegetables with the stock, seasoning and herbs. Bring to the boil, remove any scum on the surface and continue to cook for about 2 hours. Remove the bay leaves and serve. Garnish each portion with a spoonful of yogurt and a sprinkling of parsley.
Calories per portion: 94 400 kJ

Iced watercress and lemon soup

Tomato consommé

Metric

25 g powdered gelatine
1 chicken stock cube
450 ml hot water
530 ml can tomato juice
1–2 × 15 ml spoons lemon juice
Angostura bitters
Salt and freshly ground black pepper

To finish:
Mint sprigs
Lemon wedges

Imperial

1 oz powdered gelatine
1 chicken stock cube
¾ pint hot water
19 fl oz can tomato juice
1–2 tablespoons lemon juice
Angostura bitters
Salt and freshly ground black pepper

To finish:
Mint sprigs
Lemon wedges

Dissolve the gelatine and the stock cube in the hot water. If this does not completely dissolve, pour into a small basin and stand in a bowl of hot water until the mixture becomes transparent. Add the tomato juice, lemon juice and a few drops of Angostura bitters. Season to taste with the salt and pepper. Leave in a cool place to set. Chop coarsely and pile into glasses. Garnish with sprigs of mint and lemon wedges.
Calories per portion: 55 200 kJ

Carrot consommé

Metric

½ kg lean beef
2 onions, peeled and sliced
2 carrots, scrubbed and sliced
4 sticks celery, scrubbed and diced
1 l stock or water
4 peppercorns
Salt
225 g carrots, cut into matchstick strips
3 × 15 ml spoons lemon juice

Imperial

1 lb lean beef
2 onions, peeled and sliced
2 carrots, scrubbed and sliced
4 sticks celery, scrubbed and diced
1¾ pints stock or water
4 peppercorns
Salt
8 oz carrots, cut into matchstick strips
3 tablespoons lemon juice

Cooking Time: 1½ hours

Mince or chop the beef very finely. Place in a pan with the onions, carrots, celery, stock and seasoning. Bring to the boil and simmer for about 1½ hours. Strain the soup, add the carrot matchsticks and lemon juice and simmer until the carrots are tender. Adjust seasoning before serving.
Calories per portion: 50 200 kJ

Iced watercress and lemon soup

Metric

2 bunches of watercress
1 onion, finely chopped
450 ml white stock
250 ml skimmed milk
Rind of 1 lemon, finely
grated
Salt and freshly ground
black pepper
142 g carton natural
yogurt

Imperial

2 bunches of watercress
1 onion, finely chopped
¾ pint white stock
½ pint skimmed milk
Rind of 1 lemon, finely
grated
Salt and freshly ground
black pepper
5 oz carton natural
yogurt

Cooking Time: 30 minutes

Wash the watercress and remove excess stalk. Chop the leaves roughly (reserving a few of the best sprigs for garnish) and put into a pan with the onion, stock, milk, grated lemon rind and seasoning to taste. Simmer gently for 30 minutes. Purée in a blender or pass through a fine sieve and allow to cool.

Stir in the yogurt, adjust the seasoning and chill. Serve topped with small sprigs of watercress.

Calories per portion: 56 200 kJ

Carrot consommé; Tomato consommé

Cock-a-leekie

Metric	Imperial
1 boiling fowl, weighing about 1¼ kg	1 boiling fowl, weighing about 2½ lb
1 l chicken stock	1¾ pints chicken stock
Salt and freshly ground black pepper	Salt and freshly ground black pepper
½ kg leeks, washed and trimmed	1 lb leeks, washed and trimmed

To finish:
1 × 15 ml spoon finely chopped parsley

To finish:
1 tablespoon finely chopped parsley

Cooking Time: 2½ to 4 hours

Wash and dry the chicken and place in a large saucepan with the stock. Season generously. Cut the leeks into wafer-thin rings and add to the chicken. Bring to the boil and simmer for 2½–3 hours until tender. Remove the chicken from the stock, carve off the meat and cut into bite-size pieces. Serve the soup with the chicken pieces in it, or alone with the chicken as a main course. Garnish with chopped parsley.
Calories per portion: 50–152 200–650 kJ

Lettuce soup

Metric	Imperial
25 g butter	1 oz butter
1 large onion, peeled and finely chopped	1 large onion, peeled and finely chopped
1 large lettuce, washed and finely shredded	1 large lettuce, washed and finely shredded
1 l chicken stock	1¾ pints chicken stock
Salt and freshly ground black pepper	Salt and freshly ground black pepper
50 ml double cream	2 fl oz double cream

To finish:
1 × 15 ml spoon finely chopped parsley

To finish:
1 tablespoon finely chopped parsley

Cooking Time: 15 minutes

Heat the butter in a saucepan, add the onion and fry gently until soft, taking care that the onion does not colour. Add the lettuce and cook in the butter for a few minutes, then add the stock and seasoning. Bring to the boil, cover and simmer for about 7 minutes.
Purée the mixture in a blender or pass through a fine sieve. Return to the saucepan. Bring to the boil, remove from the heat and gradually add the cream. Serve hot sprinkled with chopped parsley.
Calories per portion: 180 750 kJ

French onion soup

Metric	Imperial
3 large onions, thinly sliced	3 large onions, thinly sliced
700 ml brown stock	1¼ pints brown stock
2 × 5 ml spoons beef extract	2 teaspoons beef extract
Salt and freshly ground black pepper	Salt and freshly ground black pepper

To finish:
50 g Edam cheese, grated

To finish:
2 oz Edam cheese, grated

Cooking Time: 30 minutes

Put the onions, stock, beef extract and seasoning into a saucepan and simmer for 30 minutes. Remove from heat, pour into individual soup bowls and top with a sprinkling of grated cheese. Serve immediately.
Calories per portion: 60 250 kJ

Mushrooms à la grecque

Metric

4 carrots, scrubbed
2 Spanish onions, peeled
and finely chopped
2 × 15 ml spoons olive oil
150 ml dry white wine
Salt and freshly ground
black pepper
Bouquet garni
225 g button mushrooms
8 tomatoes, skinned and
deseeded

To finish:
4 × 15 ml spoons finely
chopped parsley

Imperial

4 carrots, scrubbed
2 Spanish onions, peeled
and finely chopped
2 tablespoons olive oil
¼ pint dry white wine
Salt and freshly ground
black pepper
Bouquet garni
8 oz button mushrooms
8 tomatoes, skinned and
deseeded

To finish:
4 tablespoons finely
chopped parsley

Cooking Time: 20 minutes

Peel and finely chop the carrots and add with the onion to the hot oil. Sauté until golden. Moisten with the wine, season to taste and add the bouquet garni. Wash the mushrooms, trim the stems and add to the onion mixture with the tomatoes and a little more wine if necessary. (There should not be too much liquid as the mushrooms will add juice during cooking.) Cook uncovered for 15–20 minutes. Remove the bouquet garni, sprinkle with chopped parsley and serve cold.
Calories per portion: 125 500 kJ

Mushrooms à la grecque; Ratatouille; Honeydew melon salad

Salmon mousse

Salmon mousse

Metric	Imperial
2 eggs, separated	2 eggs, separated
2 × 5 ml spoons lemon juice	2 teaspoons lemon juice
Salt and freshly ground black pepper	Salt and freshly ground black pepper
2 × 5 ml spoons powdered gelatine	2 teaspoons powdered gelatine
225 g fresh or canned salmon	8 oz fresh or canned salmon
Cucumber slices	Cucumber slices
Lemon slices	Lemon slices

Beat the egg yolks with the lemon juice and seasoning over hot water until they thicken slightly. Allow to cool, still beating. Dissolve the gelatine in 150 ml (¼ pint) hot water and add to the egg mixture. Flake the salmon and add, folding in gently. Whisk the egg whites until stiff and fold into the salmon mixture. Pour into individual fish moulds (or one large-size one) and chill for about 2 hours. Remove from moulds and garnish with the cucumber and lemon slices.
Calories per portion: 165 650 kJ

Ratatouille

Metric	Imperial
2 large onions	2 large onions
½ kg tomatoes	1 lb tomatoes
Salt and freshly ground black pepper	Salt and freshly ground black pepper
4–6 courgettes	4–6 courgettes
4 small aubergines	4 small aubergines
1 red pepper	1 red pepper
1 green pepper	1 green pepper
1 × 15 ml spoon olive oil	1 tablespoon olive oil
1–2 cloves garlic, crushed	1–2 cloves garlic, crushed
1 sprig thyme	1 sprig thyme
2 bay leaves	2 bay leaves

Cooking Time: 1 hour

Peel and slice the onions. Skin the tomatoes, cut in half, sprinkle with salt and leave upside down to drain. Wash and thickly slice the courgettes. Remove the stalks from the aubergines, cut them in half, scoop out slightly and cut into chunks. Sprinkle with salt and leave to drain. Halve, seed, core and slice the peppers.
Heat the olive oil in a non-stick heavy-based pan and gently sauté the onion and garlic. Add all the vegetables, thyme and bay leaves and season well. Cover with a tight-fitting lid and simmer slowly until the vegetables are tender—about 1 hour. Serve hot or cold garnished with parsley.
Calories per portion: 90 400 kJ

Honeydew melon salad

Metric	Imperial
1 honeydew melon	1 honeydew melon
1 large fresh pineapple	1 large fresh pineapple
4 × 15 ml spoons Cointreau or Curaçao	4 tablespoons Cointreau or Curaçao
To finish:	To finish:
Few fresh cherries	Few fresh cherries

Slice the melon in half lengthwise, scoop out and discard the seeds. Scoop out the flesh in large pieces and keep to one side. Using scissors or a very sharp knife serrate the edge of one of the melon halves to give a decorative edge. Peel and core the pineapple and dice into chunks. Pile these and the melon pieces into the decorated melon half. Sprinkle over the liqueur and garnish with the washed and stoned cherries. Chill before serving.
Calories per portion: 102 400 kJ

Smoky roe pâté

Smoky roe pâté

Metric

1 slice stale low-calorie
bread
1 × 15 ml spoon finely
chopped parsley
225 g smoked cod's roe
1 clove garlic, crushed
15 g low-calorie spread
1 × 15 ml spoon lemon
juice
Salt and freshly ground
black pepper
Few leaves of lettuce,
shredded

To finish:
Lemon slices
Parsley sprigs

Imperial

1 slice stale low-calorie
bread
1 tablespoon finely
chopped parsley
8 oz smoked cod's roe
1 clove garlic, crushed
½ oz low-calorie spread
1 tablespoon lemon
juice
Salt and freshly ground
black pepper
Few leaves of lettuce,
shredded

To finish:
Lemon slices
Parsley sprigs

Remove the crusts from the bread and put into a blender,
on medium speed, for about ½ minute. Add the chopped
parsley, smoked cod's roe, garlic, spread and lemon juice
and blend until smooth. Remove from the blender and
season to taste.
Place a little of the lettuce in the bottom of 4 individual
ramekin dishes. Pipe rosettes of the cod's roe mixture on
top. Garnish with lemon slices and sprigs of parsley.
Calories per portion: 97 400 kJ

Minted grapefruit

Metric

2 large grapefruit
2 oranges
1 × 15 ml spoon lemon juice
*241 ml bottle low-
calorie lemonade*
*2 × 15 ml spoons finely
chopped fresh mint*

To finish:
4 mint sprigs

Imperial

2 large grapefruit
2 oranges
1 tablespoon lemon juice
*8½ fl oz bottle low-
calorie lemonade*
*2 tablespoons finely
chopped fresh mint*

To finish:
4 mint sprigs

Halve the grapefruit, using a zig-zag cut to give a decorative edge. Remove the flesh from the halves. Peel and segment the oranges, remove the membranes and cut the segments into pieces. Mix with the grapefruit and return to the grapefruit shells.

Mix together the lemon juice, lemonade and chopped mint. Pour into an icetray and freeze to soft stage. Pile on top of the grapefruit and decorate with a sprig of mint.

Calories per portion: 56 200 kJ

Minted grapefruit

23

Stuffed tomatoes

Metric

½ kg can pink salmon,
drained
1 medium stick celery,
scrubbed and chopped
2 × 15 ml spoons finely
chopped onion
2 × 15 ml spoons finely
chopped green pepper
3 × 15 ml spoons Slimmer's
French Dressing (page 71)
Salt and freshly ground
black pepper
4 large tomatoes
Lettuce

To finish:
4 lemon slices

Imperial

1 lb can pink salmon,
drained
1 medium stick celery,
scrubbed and chopped
2 tablespoons finely
chopped onion
2 tablespoons finely
chopped green pepper
3 tablespoons Slimmer's
French Dressing (page 71)
Salt and freshly ground
black pepper
4 large tomatoes
Lettuce

To finish:
4 lemon slices

Flake the salmon into a bowl, removing bones and skin. Add the celery, onion, green pepper, dressing and seasoning to taste. Mix well and chill. With stem end down, divide each tomato into six wedges, cutting down to, but not through, the base. Spread wedges apart slightly and sprinkle lightly with salt. Spoon equal amounts of the salmon mixture into the centre of each tomato. Serve on individual lettuce-lined dishes, garnished with a twist of lemon.
Calories per portion: 185 750 kJ

Avocado dip

Metric

1 clove garlic, grated or
chopped
50 g Danish Blue cheese,
grated
2 × 15 ml spoons lemon
juice
2 very ripe avocado pears,
peeled
½ teaspoon chilli powder
1 × 5 ml spoon
Worcestershire sauce
Salt and freshly ground
black pepper

To finish:
1 × 5 ml spoon finely
chopped parsley

Imperial

1 clove garlic, grated or
chopped
2 oz Danish Blue cheese,
grated
2 tablespoons lemon
juice
2 very ripe avocado pears,
peeled
½ teaspoon chilli powder
1 teaspoon
Worcestershire sauce
Salt and freshly ground
black pepper

To finish:
1 teaspoon finely
chopped parsley

Combine all the ingredients except parsley and beat well with a spoon. Season to taste with salt and pepper. Use immediately, as this mixture tends to darken very quickly. Sprinkle with chopped parsley and serve with pieces of chopped vegetables.
Calories per portion: 177 750 kJ

Slimmer's dip

Metric

175 g can crabmeat
142 g carton natural
yogurt
Salt and freshly ground
black pepper

To finish:
Lemon slices
Parsley sprigs

Imperial

6 oz can crabmeat
5 oz carton natural
yogurt
Salt and freshly ground
black pepper

To finish:
Lemon slices
Parsley sprigs

Combine the crabmeat and the yogurt, seasoning to taste. Place in a small dish and chill. Garnish just before serving with the lemon slices and parsley sprigs. Serve with slices and chunks of chopped vegetables.
Calories per portion: 71 300 kJ

Stuffed tomatoes; Slimmer's dip; Chicken and mushroom pâté; Avocado dip

Chicken and mushroom pâté

Metric

225 g cooked chicken
2 × 15 ml spoons lemon juice
½ onion, finely grated
1 × 15 ml spoon finely chopped parsley
142 g carton natural yogurt
25 g low-calorie spread
100 g mushrooms, cleaned
Salt and feshly ground black pepper

To finish:
Lemon slices
Parsley sprigs

Imperial

8 oz cooked chicken
2 tablespoons lemon juice
½ onion, finely grated
1 tablespoon finely chopped parsley
5 oz carton natural yogurt
1 oz low-calorie spread
4 oz mushrooms, cleaned
Salt and freshly ground black pepper

To finish:
Lemon slices
Parsley sprigs

Dice the chicken and blend with the lemon juice in a liquidiser, on the lowest speed, until well chopped. Add the onion, parsley, yogurt and spread and blend well together. Remove from liquidiser, add the mushrooms, sliced, and season to taste. Turn out into a small pâté or terrine dish. Chill thoroughly before serving. Garnish with lemon slices and sprigs of parsley.

Calories per portion: 84–124 300–500 kJ

Baked stuffed haddock fillet

Metric	Imperial
2 haddock fillets, each weighing 350 g	2 haddock fillets, each weighing 12 oz
2 slices low-calorie bread, made into crumbs	2 slices low-calorie bread, made into crumbs
3 × 15 ml spoons finely chopped parsley	3 tablespoons finely chopped parsley
$\frac{1}{2}$ teaspoon finely grated lemon rind	$\frac{1}{2}$ teaspoon finely grated lemon rind
$\frac{1}{2}$ teaspoon thyme	$\frac{1}{2}$ teaspoon thyme
$\frac{1}{2}$ teaspoon salt	$\frac{1}{2}$ teaspoon salt
White pepper	White pepper
40 g butter, melted	$1\frac{1}{2}$ oz butter, melted
Milk	Milk
2 large tomatoes	2 large tomatoes

Cooking Time: 40 minutes
Oven: 180°C, 350°F, Gas Mark 4

Wash and dry the fish and place one fillet, skin side down, in a shallow heatproof dish, well buttered. Make a stuffing by combining the breadcrumbs with one third of the parsley, lemon rind, thyme and seasoning and binding loosely with a third butter and a little milk. Cover the fish with the stuffing. Put the second fillet skin side uppermost on top of the stuffing. Arrange a line of tomato slices along the centre. Sprinkle with remaining parsley. Coat with the remaining melted butter and bake, uncovered, in the centre of a moderate oven for 40 minutes. Serve hot.
Calories per portion: 275 1,150 kJ

Poached whiting in piquant parsley sauce

Metric	Imperial
4 whiting fillets	4 whiting fillets
2 × 142 g cartons natural yogurt	2 × 5 oz cartons natural yogurt
2 × 5 ml spoons prepared mustard	2 teaspoons prepared mustard
4 × 5 ml spoons lemon juice	4 teaspoons lemon juice
Salt and freshly ground black pepper	Salt and freshly ground black pepper
4 × 15 ml spoons finely chopped parsley	4 tablespoons finely chopped parsley
To finish:	To finish:
Lemon slices	Lemon slices

Cooking Time: 12 minutes

Wash and wipe the fish and poach in a little water or stock until tender. Meanwhile mix together the yogurt, mustard and lemon juice in a small bowl. Heat over a saucepan of hot water—but do not allow to boil. Season to taste and stir in the chopped parsley. Spoon over the cooked fish and garnish with the lemon slices.
Calories per portion: 145 550 kJ

Prawn courgettes

Metric	Imperial
8 medium courgettes	8 medium courgettes
225 g peeled prawns	8 oz peeled prawns
1 × 15 ml spoon lemon juice	1 tablespoon lemon juice
Freshly ground black pepper	Freshly ground black pepper
25 g cottage cheese	1 oz cottage cheese
1 × 15 ml spoon lemon juice	1 tablespoon lemon juice
1–2 drops liquid sweetener	1–2 drops liquid sweetener
Salt	Salt

Cooking Time: 5 minutes

Wash and trim the courgettes, then remove a thin slice lengthways from each one. Scoop out the seeds and blanch the courgettes for 3–4 minutes in boiling water. Cool and chill. Fill with the prawns and sprinkle with the lemon juice and pepper. Mix together the cottage cheese, lemon juice and sweetener and season to taste with salt and pepper. When smooth top each courgette with a little of the cheese mixture.
Calories per portion: 100 400 kJ

Soused herrings

Metric	Imperial
4 herrings, gutted and cleaned	4 herrings, gutted and cleaned
Juice of 3 lemons	Juice of 3 lemons
6 × 15 ml spoons dry white wine	6 tablespoons dry white wine
300 ml water	½ pint water
1 onion, peeled and finely sliced	1 onion, peeled and finely sliced
6 peppercorns	6 peppercorns
2 bay leaves	2 bay leaves
½ teaspoon salt	½ teaspoon salt

Cooking Time: 45 minutes
Oven: 180°C, 350°F, Gas Mark 4

Roll the herrings from the head to the tail and place in an ovenproof dish. Pour over the lemon juice, white wine and water and add the onion and seasonings. Cover and bake for 45 minutes in a moderate oven. When the fish is cooked remove the peppercorns and bay leaves. Strain the stock, then pour it back over the herrings. Serve cold, topped with the bayleaves and sliced onions.
Calories per portion: 270 1,100 kJ

Scampi provençale

Metric	Imperial
1 × 15 ml spoon oil	1 tablespoon oil
1 small onion, peeled and finely chopped	1 small onion, peeled and finely chopped
1 clove garlic, finely chopped	1 clove garlic, finely chopped
3 tomatoes, peeled and finely chopped	3 tomatoes, peeled and finely chopped
½ kg scampi	1 lb scampi
Chopped parsley	Chopped parsley
Little white wine	Little white wine
Salt and freshly ground black pepper	Salt and freshly ground black pepper
Lemon slices (optional)	Lemon slices (optional)
Parsley sprigs (optional)	Parsley sprigs (optional)

Cooking Time: 10 minutes

Heat the oil and sauté the onion and garlic in it. Add the tomatoes, scampi, parsley and white wine to moisten. Cook steadily for 5–6 minutes. Season to taste and serve hot, garnished with lemon slices and parsley sprigs if liked.
Calories per portion: 170 700 kJ

Soused herrings; Scampi provençale

Trout in Chablis

Metric

4 medium-sized trout,
each weighing about 175 g
Salt and freshly ground
black pepper
175 ml Chablis wine
15 g butter
25 g flour

To finish:
Lemon quarters
Parsley sprigs

Imperial

4 medium-sized trout,
each weighing about 6 oz
Salt and freshly ground
black pepper
6 fl oz Chablis wine
½ oz butter
1 oz flour

To finish:
Lemon quarters
Parsley sprigs

Cooking Time: 15 minutes
Oven: 180°C, 350°F, Gas Mark 4

Wash and clean the trout, remove the backbones and put trout into a shallow casserole. Season well and pour over the wine. Bake in the centre of a moderate oven for about 15 minutes. Lift on to a hot serving dish. Melt the butter in a small saucepan, stir in the flour and cook for several minutes. Gradually add the wine left from cooking the fish. Heat for a few minutes, then pour over the fish. Garnish with lemon quarters and sprigs of parsley.

Calories per portion: 250 1,050 kJ

Trout in Chablis

Grilled salmon with slimmer's mayonnaise; Cod en cocotte

Cod en cocotte

Metric	Imperial
4 small onions, peeled and finely chopped	4 small onions, peeled and finely chopped
25 g butter	1 oz butter
4 cod cutlets (each weighing 175 g)	4 cod cutlets (each weighing 6 oz)
4 large tomatoes, peeled and sliced	4 large tomatoes, peeled and sliced
Salt and freshly ground black pepper	Salt and freshly ground black pepper
25 g Cheddar cheese, finely grated	1 oz Cheddar cheese, finely grated

To finish:
Lemon slices
Parsley sprigs

To finish:
Lemon slices
Parsley sprigs

Cooking Time: 30 minutes
Oven: 180°C, 350°F, Gas Mark 4

Fry the onion gently in the melted butter, then divide between four small individual ovenproof dishes. Place the cod cutlet on top with the slices of tomato. Season lightly and sprinkle with the grated cheese. Bake in the centre of a moderate oven until the fish is cooked. Serve garnished with the lemon slices and parsley sprigs.

Calories per portion: 216 850 kJ

Devilled crab

Metric	Imperial
4 small crabs	4 small crabs
3 slices of low-calorie bread, made into crumbs	3 slices of low-calorie bread, made into crumbs
25 g butter	1 oz butter
Pinch of salt	Pinch of salt
Pinch of cayenne pepper	Pinch of cayenne pepper
$\frac{1}{2}$–1 × 5 ml spoon curry powder	$\frac{1}{2}$–1 teaspoon curry powder
1 × 5 ml spoon Worcestershire sauce	1 teaspoon Worcestershire sauce

To finish:
Parsley sprigs
Lemon slices

To finish:
Watercress sprigs
Lemon quarters

Cooking Time: 5 minutes

Wash the crabs and remove all meat from the large claws and body—save the tiny claws for garnish. Flake the crab meat and mix with the crumbs from one slice of bread. Meanwhile sauté the remaining crumbs in the butter until well coated but not brown. Flavour the crab meat with the seasonings and return to the cleaned and polished shells. Top with the buttered crumbs. Place under a moderately hot grill until golden. Garnish with crabmeat from the small claws, watercress sprigs and lemon quarters.

Calories per portion: 190 800 kJ

Grilled salmon with slimmer's mayonnaise

Metric

*4 steaks of salmon, each
weighing 125 g*
*2 × 15 ml spoons lemon
juice*
*25 g low-calorie spread,
melted*
*Salt and freshly ground
black pepper*
*4 × 15 ml spoons Slimmer's
Mayonnaise (page 69)*

To finish:
Lemon quarters
Parsley sprigs

Imperial

*4 steaks of salmon, each
weighing 4 oz*
*2 tablespoons lemon
juice*
*1 oz low-calorie spread,
melted*
*Salt and freshly ground
black pepper*
*4 tablespoons Slimmer's
Mayonnaise (page 69)*

To finish:
Lemon quarters
Parsley sprigs

Cooking Time: 10 minutes

Preheat grill until moderately hot. Sprinkle the salmon steaks with lemon juice and brush with a little of the melted spread. Season with salt and freshly ground black pepper. Cook for 2–3 minutes and then turn. Season the second side of the steak, sprinkle with lemon juice and brush with the remainder of the melted spread. Cook for 2–3 minutes, then lower the heat and cook for a further 4 minutes to ensure the fish is cooked through to the centre. Serve with Slimmer's Mayonnaise, garnished with lemon quarters and parsley sprigs.
Calories per portion: 262 1,100 kJ

Devilled crab

Fish in a parcel

Metric

4 haddock cutlets, each
weighing 175 g
2 green peppers, washed,
deseeded and sliced
4 tomatoes, peeled and
thinly sliced
225 g mushrooms, cleaned
and finely sliced
225 g celery, scrubbed and
finely sliced
4 × 15 ml spoons lemon
juice
Salt and freshly ground
black pepper

To finish:
1 × 15 ml spoon finely
chopped parsley

Imperial

4 haddock cutlets, each
weighing 6 oz
2 green peppers, washed,
deseeded and sliced
4 tomatoes, peeled and
thinly sliced
8 oz mushrooms, cleaned
and finely sliced
8 oz celery, scrubbed and
finely sliced
4 tablespoons lemon
juice
Salt and freshly ground
black pepper

To finish:
1 tablespoon finely
.chopped parsley

Cooking Time: 40 minutes
Oven: 180°C, 350°F, Gas Mark 4

Wash the haddock, dry and place each cutlet on a piece of aluminium foil large enough to wrap around the fish. Poach the peppers, tomatoes, mushrooms and celery in the lemon juice for about 10 minutes, then pile equal quantities on top of each fish cutlet. Season to taste, wrap up the parcels and place on a baking sheet. Bake in the oven for about 30 minutes, remove from foil and garnish with the finely chopped parsley.
Calories per portion: 180 750 kJ

Grilled sole with grapes

Metric

4 lemon soles, cleaned
1 × 15 ml spoon oil
Salt and freshly ground
black pepper
4 × 15 ml spoons lemon
juice

To finish:
100 g green grapes,
peeled and depipped
Parsley sprigs
Lemon slices

Imperial

4 lemon soles, cleaned
1 tablespoon oil
Salt and freshly ground
black pepper
4 tablespoons lemon
juice

To finish:
4 oz green grapes,
peeled and depipped
Parsley sprigs
Lemon slices

Cooking Time: 10 minutes

Brush the soles very lightly with the oil, sprinkle with salt and pepper. Cook under a moderate grill for 8–10 minutes, turning once. Pour a little of the lemon juice over each sole and serve garnished with the grapes, parsley and lemon butterflies.
Calories per portion: 168 700 kJ

Halibut and cucumber mornay

Metric

4 halibut steaks, each
weighing 100 g
Salt and freshly ground
black pepper
6 peppercorns
Parsley sprig
150 ml dry cider
½ cucumber, peeled and
diced
150 ml cultured buttermilk
50 g Cheddar cheese,
grated
2 slices low-calorie bread,
made into crumbs

To finish:
Cucumber slices

Imperial

4 halibut steaks, each
weighing 4 oz
Salt and freshly ground
black pepper
6 peppercorns
Parsley sprig
¼ pint dry cider
½ cucumber, peeled and
diced
¼ pint cultured buttermilk
2 oz Cheddar cheese,
grated
2 slices low-calorie bread,
made into crumbs

To finish:
Cucumber slices

Cooking Time: 35 minutes
Oven: 180°C, 350°F, Gas Mark 4

Wash the steaks. Place in an ovenproof dish with seasoning to taste, the peppercorns and parsley. Pour over the cider, cover with foil and bake in the centre of a moderate oven for about 20 minutes. Meanwhile simmer the cucumber in the buttermilk, with a little seasoning, for about 10 minutes. When the fish is cooked, remove the peppercorns and parsley and pour the cucumber mixture over the fish. Mix the cheese and breadcrumbs together and sprinkle over fish. Grill until golden. Garnish with slices of cucumber.
Calories per portion: 230 1,000 kJ

Moules marinières

Moules marinières

Metric	Imperial
1 l mussels	*2 pints mussels*
1 small onion, peeled and finely chopped	*1 small onion, peeled and finely chopped*
2 sticks celery, scrubbed	*2 sticks celery, scrubbed*
Salt and freshly ground black pepper	*Salt and freshly ground black pepper*
1 bunch parsley	*1 bunch parsley*
1 × 15 ml spoon tarragon vinegar	*1 tablespoon tarragon vinegar*
2 × 15 ml spoons white wine	*2 tablespoons white wine*

Cooking Time: 10 minutes

Scrub the mussels well, discarding any that are open and will not close when tapped sharply. Put into a large pan with enough water to cover. Add the onion, chopped celery, seasoning and parsley. Heat until the mussels open. Remove beards from the mussels and leave mussels on half shell. Reboil the liquid with the vinegar and wine and strain over the mussels.

Calories per portion: 40 150 kJ

Monks' mackerel

Monks'mackerel

Metric	Imperial
4 medium mackerel, cleaned and gutted	*4 medium mackerel, cleaned and gutted*
2 onions, peeled and chopped	*2 onions, peeled and chopped*
2 bay leaves	*2 bay leaves*
4 × 15 ml spoons lemon juice	*4 tablespoons lemon juice*
2 × 5 ml spoons dried mixed herbs	*2 teaspoons dried mixed herbs*
12 black olives	*12 black olives*
Salt and freshly ground black pepper	*Salt and freshly ground black pepper*

To finish:
Watercress sprigs
Lemon wedges

To finish:
Watercress sprigs
Lemon wedges

Cooking Time: 30–40 minutes
Oven: 180°C, 350°F, Gas Mark 4

Place the mackerel on a non-stick baking dish and cover with the onion, bay leaves, lemon juice, herbs and stoned olives. Season well with salt and pepper. Cover with foil and bake for 30–40 minutes until the fish is cooked. Serve hot with the watercress sprigs and lemon wedges as a garnish.
Calories per portion: 198 800 kJ

Beef stroganoff

Metric	Imperial
½ kg rump or fillet steak	1 lb rump or fillet steak
1 onion, peeled and finely sliced	1 onion, peeled and finely sliced
25 g butter	1 oz butter
225 g mushrooms, finely sliced	8 oz mushrooms, finely sliced
Salt and freshly ground black pepper	Salt and freshly ground black pepper
142 g carton soured cream	5 oz carton soured cream
142 g carton natural yogurt	5 oz carton natural yogurt

To finish:
Finely chopped parsley

To finish:
Finely chopped parsley

Cooking Time: 10 minutes

Beat the steak, trim and cut into strips. Sauté the onion in the butter in a non-stick pan until golden brown—about 5 minutes. Add the mushrooms and cook for 3–4 minutes. Season to taste, add the beef and cook for 5–7 minutes. Mix together the soured cream and the yogurt. Stir into the beef mixture and warm gently. Serve with a little boiled rice and a salad sprinkled with finely chopped parsley.
Calories per portion: 450 1,800 kJ

Beef stroganoff

Minted crown roast of lamb

Metric

2 best end necks of lamb,
with 6–8 chops, shaped
into a crown
Salt and freshly ground
black pepper
25 g dried apricots, soaked
overnight
50 g low-calorie bread-
crumbs
½ cooking apple, peeled,
cored and chopped
1 × 15 ml spoon walnuts,
chopped
1 × 15 ml spoon finely
grated lemon rind
25 g butter, melted

To finish:
Apricot halves
Mint jelly

Imperial

2 best end necks of lamb,
with 6–8 chops, shaped
into a crown
Salt and freshly ground
black pepper
1 oz dried apricots, soaked
overnight
2 oz low-calorie bread-
crumbs
½ cooking apple, peeled,
cored and chopped
1 tablespoon walnuts,
chopped
1 tablespoon finely
grated lemon rind
1 oz butter, melted

To finish:
Apricot halves
Mint jelly

Cooking Time: $1\frac{1}{4}$–$1\frac{1}{2}$ hours
Oven: 190°C, 375°F, Gas Mark 5

Place the crown roast in a large roasting pan. Season generously and wrap a small piece of foil round the top of each rib to prevent scorching. To prepare stuffing, snip dried apricots into small pieces and combine with the breadcrumbs, apple, walnuts and grated lemon rind. Mix with the melted butter. Pack stuffing into the middle of the crown and cover with a circle of foil. Cook in the centre of a moderately hot oven for $1\frac{1}{4}$–$1\frac{1}{2}$ hours. When cooked remove pieces of foil and top each rib with a cutlet frill. Garnish with apricot halves filled with mint jelly.
Serves 6–8.
Calories per portion: 375 1,600 kJ

Minted crown roast of lamb

Spring lamb stew

Metric	Imperial
½ kg lean stewing lamb, trimmed free of fat	1 lb lean stewing lamb, trimmed free of fat
700 ml water	1¼ pints water
Bouquet garni	Bouquet garni
Salt and freshly ground black pepper	Salt and freshly ground black pepper
8 spring onions, washed and trimmed	8 spring onions, washed and trimmed
8 small carrots, scrubbed and trimmed	8 small carrots, scrubbed and trimmed
350 g fresh peas, shelled	12 oz fresh peas, shelled
350 g broad beans, shelled	12 oz broad beans, shelled
4 eggs	4 eggs
2 × 15 ml spoons lemon juice	2 tablespoons lemon juice

To finish:	To finish:
1 × 15 ml spoon finely chopped parsley	1 tablespoon finely chopped parsley

Cooking Time: 1 hour 40 minutes

Cut the lamb into serving-size pieces and place in a pan with the water and bouquet garni. Season generously, bring to the boil and simmer for 1 hour. Add the onions, carrots, peas and beans and simmer for a further 30 minutes.

Whisk the eggs lightly with the lemon juice. Strain off the liquid from the lamb, discard the bouquet garni and cool slightly. Whisk the liquid slowly into the egg mixture and return to the pan containing the meat and vegetables. Heat, without boiling, until the mixture is thick, stirring continuously. Taste and adjust seasoning. Turn into a serving dish and garnish with the chopped parsley. Serve with a green salad.

Calories per portion: 490 2,000 kJ

Burgundy beef

Metric	Imperial
1 × 15 ml spoon olive oil	1 tablespoon olive oil
1 large onion, peeled and sliced	1 large onion, peeled and sliced
2 green peppers, washed and deseeded	2 green peppers, washed and deseeded
½ kg chuck steak	1 lb chuck steak
150 ml burgundy	¼ pint burgundy
2 × 15 ml spoons tomato purée	2 tablespoons tomato purée
Salt and freshly ground black pepper	Salt and freshly ground black pepper
1 packet frozen corn kernels	1 packet frozen corn kernels

Cooking Time: 1½–2 hours
Oven: 180°C, 350°F, Gas Mark 4

Heat the oil in a non-stick frying pan, add the onion and fry lightly. Cut the flesh of the peppers into thin strips and add to the onion. Wash and trim the meat, and cut into 2.5 cm (1 in) cubes. Add to the vegetables and sauté lightly. Stir in the burgundy and tomato purée. Put the contents of the pan into a lidded casserole and season to taste. Simmer gently in a moderate oven for 1½–2 hours. Add the corn kernels and cook for a further 15 minutes. Adjust seasoning and serve.

Calories per portion: 407 1,650 kJ

Green pepper steak

Metric	Imperial
4 rump steaks each weighing about 100–175 g	4 rump steaks each weighing about 4–6 oz
2 × 15 ml cooking oil	2 tablespoons cooking oil
396 g can tomatoes	14 oz can tomatoes
½ medium onion, finely sliced	½ medium onion, finely sliced
1 small clove garlic, finely chopped	1 small clove garlic, finely chopped
1 × 5 ml spoon beef extract	1 teaspoon beef extract
1 × 5 ml spoon Worcestershire sauce	1 teaspoon Worcestershire sauce
Salt and freshly ground black pepper	Salt and freshly ground black pepper
2 small green peppers, deseeded and sliced	2 small green peppers, deseeded and sliced

Cooking Time: 1 hour 10 minutes

Trim any excess fat from the steaks and cut into strips 5 cm by 1.5 cm (2 in by ½ in). Heat the oil in a heavy-based frying pan and brown the meat on all sides. Drain off excess fat. Drain the tomatoes, reserving the liquid. Add the reserved tomato liquid, onion slices, garlic, beef extract, Worcestershire sauce and seasoning to taste to the browned strips of meat. Cover tightly and simmer over a low heat for 50 minutes. Stir in the green pepper strips and drained tomatoes. Cook, covered, till peppers are tender—about 6–8 minutes. Remove meat and vegetables to a serving bowl using a slotted spoon. Make up pan juices to 150 ml (¼ pint) with boiling water and pour over steak. Serve with a salad and a little boiled rice.

Calories per portion: 385 1,600 kJ

Green pepper steak; Spring lamb stew; Burgundy beef

French beef and olive casserole

Metric	Imperial
350 g rump, blade or chuck steak	12 oz rump, blade or chuck steak
1 × 15 ml spoon olive oil	1 tablespoon olive oil
1 carrot, scrubbed and sliced	1 carrot, scrubbed and sliced
1 onion, peeled and sliced	1 onion, peeled and sliced
3 sticks celery, scrubbed and cut into 2.5 cm pieces	3 sticks celery, scrubbed and cut into 1 in pieces
150 ml red wine	¼ pint red wine
4 × 15 ml spoons wine vinegar	4 tablespoons wine vinegar
Bouquet garni	Bouquet garni
1 clove garlic, crushed	1 clove garlic, crushed
Few peppercorns	Few peppercorns
Salt and freshly ground black pepper	Salt and freshly ground black pepper
100 g lean bacon, diced	4 oz lean bacon, diced
100 g green olives	4 oz green olives
3 tomatoes, skinned and sliced	3 tomatoes, skinned and sliced

Cooking Time: 1¾–2¾ hours
Oven: 160°C, 325°F, Gas Mark 3

Trim the meat and cut into thick chunks. Make a marinade by heating the oil and cooking the carrot, onion and celery in this until brown. Add half the wine, the vinegar, bouquet garni, garlic and peppercorns; season to taste. Bring to the boil and simmer for 15 minutes. Cool slightly and put in the meat to marinate for 1–2 hours.

Fry the bacon and remove from the pan, then fry the drained meat on both sides and put into an earthenware casserole. Add the strained marinade, bacon, remaining wine and olives. Cover with greaseproof paper and then the lid, and cook in a slow oven for 1½–2½ hours. Shortly before serving skim off any excess fat and add the tomatoes. Serve with a salad and a few cooked noodles.

Calories per portion: 430 1,750 kJ

Lamb's liver with thyme

Metric	Imperial
½ kg lamb's liver, thinly sliced	1 lb lamb's liver, thinly sliced
25 g seasoned flour	1 oz seasoned flour
2 × 15 ml spoon finely chopped fresh thyme (or 1 × 5 ml spoon dried)	2 tablespoons finely chopped fresh thyme (or 1 teaspoon dried)
25 g butter	1 oz butter

To finish:
Baked tomatoes
Watercress

To finish:
Baked tomatoes
Watercress

Cooking Time: 10 minutes

Lightly coat the thin liver slices in the seasoned flour. Sprinkle with half of the thyme. Melt the butter in a heavy-based pan and gently cook the liver slices in this until cooked—about 10 minutes. Remove on to a heated serving dish. Sprinkle the remaining thyme into the pan juices and pour over the liver. Garnish with baked tomatoes and watercress.

Calories per portion: 220 900 kJ

Filet mignon

Metric	Imperial
4 lean rashers bacon	4 lean rashers bacon
4 × 150 g pieces of fillet steak, 2.5 cm thick	4 × 5 oz pieces of fillet steak, 1 in thick
Salt and freshly ground black pepper	Salt and freshly ground black pepper
225 g mushrooms, cleaned	8 oz mushrooms, cleaned
150 ml stock	¼ pint stock
1 × 15 ml spoon lemon juice	1 tablespoon lemon juice

To finish:
Grilled tomatoes
Watercress

To finish:
Grilled tomatoes
Watercress

Cooking Time: 8–12 minutes

Wrap a lean rasher of bacon around the edge of each fillet steak, securing with a cocktail stick. Season and grill under a moderate heat for 8–12 minutes or until steak is cooked to required state. Meanwhile poach the mushrooms in the stock and lemon juice until tender. Serve with the cooked steak, garnished with grilled tomatoes and watercress.

Calories per portion: 440 1,750 kJ

French beef and olive casserole; Filet mignon; Lamb's liver with thyme

Dolmas

Metric	Imperial
350 g minced beef	12 oz minced beef
1 onion, peeled and finely chopped	1 onion, peeled and finely chopped
50 g mushrooms, washed, peeled and sliced	2 oz mushrooms, washed, peeled and sliced
1 tomato, skinned and finely chopped	1 tomato, skinned and finely chopped
1 × 5 ml spoon oregano	1 teaspoon oregano
1 × 15 ml spoon tomato purée	1 tablespoon tomato purée
Salt and freshly ground black pepper	Salt and freshly ground black pepper
8 cabbage leaves, washed and trimmed	8 cabbage leaves, washed and trimmed
250 ml tomato juice	8 fl oz tomato juice
1 × 5 ml spoon cornflour	1 teaspoon cornflour
Few drops Worcestershire sauce	Few drops Worcestershire sauce
1 × 15 ml spoon finely chopped mint	1 tablespoon finely chopped mint

To finish:
Tomato slices

To finish:
Tomato slices

Cooking Time: 1 hour 10 minutes
Oven: 180°C, 350°F, Gas Mark 4

In a non-stick frying pan cook the minced beef, onion and mushrooms until brown—about 4 minutes. Stir in the tomato, oregano and tomato purée; season to taste. Blanch the cabbage leaves in boiling, salted water for 3–4 minutes and drain. Divide the meat mixture between the cabbage leaves and roll up. (Secure with cocktail sticks if wished.)
Blend together the tomato juice and cornflour. Place in a small saucepan and bring to the boil, stirring. Add the Worcestershire sauce and chopped mint. Pour half the sauce into an ovenproof dish. Arrange stuffed cabbage leaves on top. Cover tightly. Bake in the centre of a moderate oven for 1 hour.
Warm the remaining sauce through and pour over the cabbage leaves. Garnish with the tomato slices.
Calories per portion: 226 950 kJ

Lamb kebabs with barbecue sauce

Metric	Imperial
½ kg lean lamb, cut into 4 cm cubes	1 lb lean lamb, cut into 1½ in cubes
8 small tomatoes, washed	8 small tomatoes, washed
12 small mushrooms, cleaned and trimmed	12 small mushrooms, cleaned and trimmed
5 × 15 ml spoons lemon juice	5 tablespoons lemon juice
5 × 15 ml spoons soy sauce	5 tablespoons soy sauce
4 × 5 ml spoons Worcestershire sauce	4 teaspoons Worcestershire sauce
1 clove garlic, crushed	1 clove garlic, crushed
50 g low-calorie spread	2 oz low-calorie spread

To finish:
4 carrots, scrubbed and grated
½ small cabbage, washed and shredded
2 small apples, washed and diced

To finish:
4 carrots, scrubbed and grated
½ small cabbage, washed and shredded
2 small apples, washed and diced

Cooking Time: 15 minutes

Thread the meat, tomatoes and mushrooms alternately on to four skewers. Put the lemon juice, soy sauce, Worcestershire sauce, garlic and spread into a small pan and heat to melt the spread. Marinate the skewered kebabs in this mixture for at least 2 hours. Cook the kebabs on a barbecue or under a hot grill for 10–15 minutes or until the meat is tender, turning and basting with the remaining sauce. Serve on a bed of shredded cabbage, carrot and apple with the remainder of the barbecue sauce.
Calories per portion: 380 1,500 kJ

Grilled steak with slimmer's sauce

Metric

4 fillet, sirloin or rump
steaks, each weighing 175 g
2 × 5 ml spoons oil

To finish:
25 g low-calorie spread
2 × 5 ml spoons finely
chopped parsley
Salt and freshly ground
black pepper
½ teaspoon lemon juice
Watercress sprigs
Grilled tomatoes

Imperial

4 fillet, sirloin or rump
steaks, each weighing 6 oz
2 teaspoons oil

To finish:
1 oz low-calorie spread
2 teaspoons finely
chopped parsley
Salt and freshly ground
black pepper
½ teaspoon lemon juice
Watercress sprigs
Grilled tomatoes

Cooking Time: 8–15 minutes

Brush the steak with the oil. Bring grill to hot and cook the steaks for one minute on each side. Reduce heat slightly and cook, turning every two minutes until cooked to desired state (the time will depend upon thickness of steak and whether you like it rare, medium or well done). Serve with parsley 'butter', watercress and grilled tomatoes.
To make the parsley 'butter' place the spread on a plate and soften slightly with a palette knife. Work in the parsley, seasoning and lemon juice, shape into a long roll and chill. Serve slices or pats on top of the hot meat just before serving.
Calories per portion: 490 2,000 kJ

Beef olives

Metric

½ kg topside
1 clove garlic (optional)
100 g ham, diced
2 carrots, scrubbed and
finely chopped
2 onions, peeled and finely
chopped
2 × 15 ml spoons tomato
purée
300 ml beef stock
Salt and freshly ground
black pepper
1 × 5 ml spoon mixed herbs

To finish:
1 × 15 ml spoon finely
chopped parsley

Imperial

1 lb topside
1 clove garlic (optional)
4 oz ham, diced
2 carrots, scrubbed and
finely chopped
2 onions, peeled and finely
chopped
2 tablespoons tomato
purée
½ pint beef stock
Salt and freshly ground
black pepper
1 teaspoon mixed herbs

To finish:
1 tablespoon finely
chopped parsley

Cooking Time: 2–3 hours
Oven: 180°C, 350°F, Gas Mark 4

Divide the steak into 4 pieces and flatten them into thin slices. Rub with the garlic if used. Mix the ham with a quarter of the carrot and onion, tomato purée, a little of the stock, seasoning and herbs. Combine well and spread this filling over the steaks. Roll them up and secure each with a skewer. Place the remaining vegetables in the bottom of a lidded casserole and put the meat on top. Pour over the remaining stock. Simmer in the oven for 2 hours or until tender. When cooked, remove and serve sprinkled with the chopped parsley.
Calories per portion: 374 1,600 kJ

Liver provençale

Metric

½ kg lamb's liver, washed
and trimmed
1 onion, finely sliced
1 green pepper, cleaned,
deseeded and sliced
1 red pepper, cleaned,
deseeded and sliced
1 clove garlic, crushed
396 g can tomatoes
Salt and freshly ground
black pepper

To finish:
1 × 15 ml chopped parsley

Imperial

1 lb lamb's liver, washed
and trimmed
1 onion, finely sliced
1 green pepper, cleaned,
deseeded and sliced
1 red pepper, cleaned,
deseeded and sliced
1 clove garlic, crushed
14 oz can tomatoes
Salt and freshly ground
black pepper

To finish:
1 tablespoon chopped parsley

Cooking Time: 1 hour
Oven: 180°C, 350°F, Gas Mark 4

Cut the liver into thin slices. Layer in a shallow casserole with the onion, green and red peppers and the garlic. Pour over the canned tomatoes and season to taste with salt and pepper. Cover and cook in a moderate oven for 1 hour. Remove, adjust seasoning and sprinkle with the finely chopped parsley.

Calories per portion: 200 800 kJ

Grilled steak with slimmer's sauce; Beef olives

Escalope of veal in paprika sauce

Metric	Imperial
1 × 15 ml spoon oil	1 tablespoon oil
½ kg veal fillet, cut in 1.5 cm slices, beaten	1 lb veal fillet, cut in ½ in slices, beaten
1 onion, peeled and thinly sliced	1 onion, peeled and thinly sliced
1 × 5 ml spoon paprika	1 teaspoon paprika
25 g flour	1 oz flour
Stock	Stock
Salt and freshly ground black pepper	Salt and freshly ground black pepper
3 × 15 ml spoons natural yogurt	3 tablespoons natural yogurt

Cooking Time: 30 minutes

Heat the oil in a non-stick pan and cook the veal on both sides until lightly browned. Lift out and keep hot. Put the onion and paprika into the pan and sauté for 3 minutes. Add the flour and mix well. Slowly add enough stock to make a thick sauce. Season to taste. Return the veal slices, cover and cook for 20 minutes. Five minutes before serving stir in the yogurt; reheat gently but do not boil. Serve with cooked noodles.

Calories per portion: 195 800 kJ

Honey roast ham with slimmer's spicy sauce

Metric	Imperial
1 kg gammon joint	2 lb gammon joint
12 cloves	12 cloves
25 g demerara sugar	1 oz demerara sugar
1 × 15 ml spoon honey	1 tablespoon honey
3 × 15 ml spoons orange juice	3 tablespoons orange juice
2 × 15 ml spoons redcurrant jelly	2 tablespoons redcurrant jelly
Rind of ½ orange, finely shredded	Rind of ½ orange, finely shredded
3 × 15 ml spoons orange juice	3 tablespoons orange juice
2 × 15 ml spoons lemon juice	2 tablespoons lemon juice
150 ml stock	¼ pint stock
To finish:	To finish:
Orange slices	Orange slices

Cooking Time: 1¼ hours
Oven: 180°C, 350°F, Gas Mark 4;
220°C, 425°F, Gas Mark 7

Soak the gammon in cold water overnight. Place in a saucepan, cover with cold water, bring to the boil, remove the scum and simmer for 30 minutes. Remove the joint and carefully strip off the skin. Score the fat and stud with cloves. Place in a baking tin. Blend the sugar, honey and orange juice and pour over the joint. Bake in a moderate oven for 45 minutes. Fifteen minutes before the end of cooking increase the temperature to hot and baste the meat. Meanwhile melt the redcurrant jelly in a small pan and add the orange rind, orange juice, lemon juice and stock. Heat and serve with the ham, garnished with orange slices.

Calories per portion: 300 1,200 kJ

Liver shashlik

Metric	Imperial
½ kg lamb's liver, cut into bite size pieces	1 lb lamb's liver, cut into bite size pieces
8 small onions, peeled and blanched	8 small onions, peeled and blanched
8 small tomatoes, peeled	8 small tomatoes, peeled
225 g mushrooms, cleaned	8 oz mushrooms, cleaned
Fresh bay leaves (optional)	Fresh bay leaves (optional)
1 × 15 ml spoon oil	1 tablespoon oil
1 × 15 ml spoon wine vinegar	1 tablespoon wine vinegar
Salt and freshly ground black pepper	Salt and freshly ground black pepper
1 lemon	1 lemon
Parsley, finely chopped	Parsley, finely chopped

Cooking Time: 10–15 minutes

Take 8 long skewers and thread with liver, onions, tomatoes, mushrooms and bay leaves. Brush lightly with the oil, sprinkle with a little vinegar and season with salt and pepper. Cook under a hot grill for about 8 minutes, turning frequently. Remove skewers. Add the juice from one lemon and a little chopped parsley to any juices in the grill pan, heat and pour over the kebabs. Serve with a little boiled rice and a salad.

Calories per portion: 225 950 kJ

Stuffed peppers

Metric	Imperial
4 medium green peppers	4 medium green peppers
Salt and freshly ground black pepper	Salt and freshly ground black pepper
225 g lean minced beef	8 oz lean minced beef
1 small onion, finely chopped	1 small onion, finely chopped
50 g mushrooms, cleaned and sliced	2 oz mushrooms, cleaned and sliced
2 tomatoes, skinned and chopped	2 tomatoes, skinned and chopped
1 slice low-calorie bread, toasted and cubed	1 slice low-calorie bread, toasted and cubed
$\frac{1}{4}$ teaspoon Worcestershire sauce	$\frac{1}{4}$ teaspoon Worcestershire sauce

Cooking Time: 35 minutes
Oven: 180°C, 350°F, Gas Mark 4

Wash and dry peppers, cut off the tops, remove seeds and membrane. Pre-cook in boiling salted water for 5 minutes and drain. Generously season the insides and tops of the peppers. In a non-stick frying pan brown the beef with the onion. Stir in the mushrooms, tomatoes, bread and Worcestershire sauce; season to taste. Spoon the mixture into the peppers and replace the top on each one. Place in a baking dish and bake in a moderate oven for about 25 minutes or until cooked.
Calories per portion: 185 750 kJ

Sweet and sour pork

Metric	Imperial
25 g butter	1 oz butter
$\frac{1}{2}$ kg lean pork fillet, cut into chunks	1 lb lean pork fillet, cut into chunks
4 onions, peeled and sliced	4 onions, peeled and sliced
500 ml beef stock	1 pint beef stock
100 g pineapple chunks, drained from syrup	4 oz pineapple chunks, drained from syrup
1 small green pepper, cleaned, deseeded and sliced	1 small green pepper, cleaned, deseeded and sliced
1 small red pepper, cleaned, deseeded and sliced	1 small red pepper, cleaned, deseeded and sliced
1 × 15 ml spoon soy sauce	1 tablespoon soy sauce

Cooking Time: 2–2$\frac{1}{2}$ hours
Oven: 160°C, 325°F, Gas Mark 3

Melt the butter in a heavy-based saucepan and brown the meat evenly. Transfer meat to an ovenproof dish, leaving surplus fat behind. Soften the onions in this and add to the meat. Add the beef stock and cook in a slow oven for 2–2$\frac{1}{2}$ hours until the meat is tender. About $\frac{1}{2}$ hour before serving add the diced pineapple chunks, green and red peppers and soy sauce. Serve in deep individual bowls.
Calories per portion: 250 1,050 kJ

Slimmer's goulash

Metric	Imperial
550 g chuck steak	1$\frac{1}{4}$ lb chuck steak
25 g seasoned flour	1 oz seasoned flour
2 × 15 ml spoons oil	2 tablespoons oil
1 onion, peeled and thinly sliced	1 onion, peeled and thinly sliced
150 ml stock	$\frac{1}{4}$ pint stock
396 g can tomatoes	14 oz can tomatoes
1 × 5 ml spoon tomato purée	1 teaspoon tomato purée
100 g peas	4 oz peas
2 × 5 ml spoons paprika	2 teaspoons paprika
2 × 15 ml spoons natural yogurt	2 tablespoons natural yogurt
Salt and freshly ground black pepper	Salt and freshly ground black pepper

Cooking Time: 1$\frac{3}{4}$ hours

Dice the meat, coat with the seasoned flour and brown quickly in the hot oil. Remove from pan and sauté the sliced onion until soft. Return the meat, add stock, tomatoes and purée, cover and simmer for 1$\frac{3}{4}$ hours. Add the peas, paprika and seasoning to taste 10 minutes before the end of cooking. Remove from the heat and stir in the yogurt. Serve immediately with a crisp salad.
Calories per portion: 520 2,100 kJ

Sweet and sour pork; Slimmer's goulash; Stuffed peppers

Cherry glazed duck

Cherry glazed duck

Metric	Imperial
1 duck, 1.8 kg dressed weight	1 duck, 4 lb dressed weight
½ kg cherries	1 lb cherries
300 ml dry white wine	½ pint dry white wine

Cooking Time: 1 hour 40 minutes
Oven: 200°C, 400°F, Gas Mark 6

Pluck, draw and truss the duck. Prick all over with a needle or fine skewer, place on a wire rack over a baking dish and cook in a hot oven, allowing 20 minutes per ½ kg (1lb) and 20 minutes over. Simmer all but 12 cherries in the wine until tender; sieve to remove skin and stones. Spoon some of this cherry sauce over the duck 20 minutes before the end of cooking and 10 minutes later. Boil the remainder rapidly to reduce by half. Serve the duck on a large dish, with the whole cherries and cherry sauce.
Calories per portion: 410 1,700 kJ

Chicken marengo

Metric	Imperial
4 chicken joints	4 chicken joints
100 g carrots, scrubbed and sliced	4 oz carrots, scrubbed and sliced
100 g mushrooms, cleaned and sliced	4 oz mushrooms, cleaned and sliced
100 g onions, peeled and chopped	4 oz onions, peeled and chopped
450 ml stock	¾ pint stock
Salt and freshly ground black pepper	Salt and freshly ground black pepper
1 × 15 ml spoon white wine	1 tablespoon white wine

Cooking Time: 1¼ hours
Oven: 180°C, 350°F, Gas Mark 4

Brown the chicken joints under a moderate grill, taking care that they do not scorch. Place in a casserole dish with the carrots, mushrooms, onions and stock. Season to taste with salt and pepper. Cover and bake for 1¼ hours. When cooked place the chicken on a serving dish. Add the wine to the liquid, boil rapidly to reduce the volume and pour over the chicken.
Calories per portion: 170 700 kJ

Chicken marengo; French rabbit terrine; Chicken with rosemary

French rabbit terrine

Metric	Imperial
1 rabbit, ready-prepared	*1 rabbit, ready-prepared*
6 slices lean bacon	*6 slices lean bacon*
Salt and freshly ground	*Salt and freshly ground*
black pepper	*black pepper*
2 eggs, beaten	*2 eggs, beaten*
2 × 15 ml spoons red wine	*2 tablespoons red wine*
Bay leaf	*Bay leaf*
1 × 5 ml spoon dried thyme	*1 teaspoon dried thyme*

Cooking Time: 1½–2 hours
Oven: 180°C, 350°F, Gas Mark 4

Cut up the rabbit, reserving the liver, and remove the flesh from the bones. Cut the white parts of the flesh into thin strips. Mince the remainder with the liver. Cut the bacon into strips and use to line a small terrine. Season the minced mixture to taste and add the eggs and wine. Place the minced mixture over the bacon, then cover with the strips of white rabbit meat and any remaining bacon. Add the bay leaf and thyme and cook in a moderate oven for 1½–2 hours until tender.
Calories per portion: 380 1,500 kJ

Chicken with rosemary

Metric	Imperial
1 roasting chicken,	*1 roasting chicken,*
weighing 1.4–1.6 kg	*weighing 3–3½ lb*
2 small rosemary sprigs	*2 small rosemary sprigs*
150 ml stock	*¼ pint stock*
Salt and freshly ground	*Salt and freshly ground*
black pepper	*black pepper*
15 g butter	*½ oz butter*
To finish:	*To finish:*
Watercress sprigs	*Watercress sprigs*
Baked tomatoes	*Baked tomatoes*

Cooking Time: 1–1¼ hours
Oven: 200°C, 400°F, Gas Mark 6

Wash the chicken and dry. Stuff the inside of the carcass with the sprigs of rosemary. Place in a roasting pan and pour in the stock. Sprinkle with the seasoning and dot with butter. Roast in a moderately hot oven for 1–1¼ hours until golden. Remove the rosemary and serve on a hot dish with a thin gravy made from the surrounding stock. Garnish with watercress and baked tomatoes.
Calories per portion: 240 950 kJ

51

Stuffed pigeons

Metric

4 ready-to-cook young pigeons
2 × 15 ml spoons lemon juice
Salt and freshly ground black pepper
12 chicken livers, trimmed
40 g butter
100 g mushrooms, cleaned and finely sliced
100 g cooked ham, diced
50 g almonds, chopped
½ teaspoon dried thyme

To finish:
Watercress

Imperial

4 ready-to-cook young pigeons
2 tablespoons lemon juice
Salt and freshly ground black pepper
12 chicken livers, trimmed
1½ oz butter
4 oz mushrooms, cleaned and finely sliced
4 oz cooked ham, diced
2 oz almonds, chopped
½ teaspoon dried thyme

To finish:
Watercress

Cooking Time: 1¼ hours
Oven: 160°C, 325°F, Gas Mark 3

Rub the inside of the body cavities of the pigeons with half of the lemon juice and season generously. Cook the chicken livers in a pan with half the butter until barely cooked. Remove and finely chop. Sauté the mushrooms in the remaining butter and add to the livers with the ham, almonds, thyme and remaining lemon juice. Season to taste. Stuff the mixture into the body cavities and truss to secure. Place the pigeons on a rack, breast side up, in a shallow baking tin. Roast in a slow oven for 1 hour or until cooked, basting occasionally with the pan drippings. Serve hot garnished with the watercress.
Calories per portion: 520 650 kJ

Roast chicken with slimmer's bread sauce

Metric

1 × 1.8 kg oven-ready chicken
Salt and freshly ground black pepper
2 × 5 ml spoons olive oil
1 onion, peeled and finely chopped
250 ml skimmed milk
3 wheat crispbreads, crushed
Pinch of ground nutmeg
Rind of half a lemon, finely grated

To finish:
Watercress sprigs

Imperial

1 × 4 lb oven-ready chicken
Salt and freshly ground black pepper
2 teaspoons olive oil
1 onion, peeled and finely chopped
½ pint skimmed milk
3 wheat crispbreads, crushed
Pinch of ground nutmeg
Rind of half a lemon, finely grated

To finish:
Watercress sprigs

Cooking Time: 1 hour 40 minutes
Oven: 190°C, 375°F, Gas Mark 5

Rinse the chicken inside and out and pat dry. Sprinkle the inside with salt and truss. Lightly rub the skin with the olive oil. Place in a shallow roasting tin and cover with foil. Roast in a moderate oven allowing 20 minutes per ½ kg (1 lb) plus 20 minutes. During the last 45 minutes turn back the foil to brown the bird.
Meanwhile simmer the chopped onion in the milk for about 10 minutes. Remove from the heat and stir in the crushed crispbreads, nutmeg and grated lemon rind. Season to taste and leave in a warm place for ½ hour. Serve the roast chicken with this bread sauce, garnished with watercress.
Calories per portion: 250 1,050 kJ

Poulet chasseur

Metric

4 chicken joints
2 carrots, scrubbed
½ turnip, peeled
½ swede, peeled
1 small onion, peeled
1 stick celery, scrubbed
1 × 15 ml spoon oil
450 ml stock
2 tomatoes, peeled
Salt and freshly ground black pepper
1 × 15 ml spoon sherry

To finish:
100 g mushrooms, cleaned
150 ml stock

Imperial

4 chicken joints
2 carrots, scrubbed
½ turnip, peeled
½ swede, peeled
1 small onion, peeled
1 stick celery, scrubbed
1 tablespoon oil
¾ pint stock
2 tomatoes, peeled
Salt and freshly ground black pepper
1 tablespoon sherry

To finish:
4 oz mushrooms, cleaned
¼ pint stock

Cooking Time: 1 hour 10 minutes

Wipe the chicken joints. Chop the vegetables into even-sized pieces and sauté lightly in a heavy-based pan in the oil. Grill the joints of chicken on both sides until golden, then place on the bed of vegetables. Add the stock, deseeded and chopped tomatoes and season to taste. Cover and simmer slowly for 1 hour. Remove the chicken and strain the sauce, keeping the vegetables hot, and simmer to reduce it. When syrupy add the sherry and adjust seasoning. Mound the vegetables on a dish and place the chicken portions on top. Pour over a little of the sauce and garnish with the mushrooms, which have been cooked in a little stock.
Calories per portion: 230 950 kJ

Stuffed pigeons; Poulet chasseur; Roast chicken with slimmer's bread sauce

Chicken paprika

Metric	Imperial
4 chicken joints, washed and dried	4 chicken joints, washed and dried
1 × 5 ml spoon salt	1 teaspoon salt
2 × 5 ml spoons paprika pepper	2 teaspoons paprika pepper
150 ml chicken stock	¼ pint chicken stock
1 onion, peeled and finely chopped	1 onion, peeled and finely chopped
142 g carton natural yogurt	5 oz carton natural yogurt
Freshly ground black pepper	Freshly ground black pepper
To finish:	To finish:
2 × 15 ml spoons finely chopped parsley	2 tablespoons finely chopped parsley

Cooking Time: 50 minutes

Sprinkle the chicken joints with the salt and paprika pepper. Put in a grill pan, without the rack, and cook for 5 minutes on each side, or until well browned. (Do not put too near the heat or they will scorch before browning.) Remove and place in a lidded casserole with 150 ml (¼ pint) chicken stock and the onion. Cover and simmer over a moderate heat for 30–40 minutes or until tender, adding more stock if necessary. Lift out the chicken, place on a warmed serving dish and keep hot. If excess liquid is present, reduce to 150 ml (¼ pint). Stir in the yogurt and adjust the seasoning. Heat slowly, stirring well, but do not allow to boil. Pour over chicken and sprinkle with chopped parsley.
Calories per portion: 220 850 kJ

Bengal chicken curry

Metric	Imperial
1 × 15 ml spoon oil	1 tablespoon oil
2 onions, peeled and chopped	2 onions, peeled and chopped
1 clove garlic, crushed	1 clove garlic, crushed
1 × 5 ml spoon dry mustard	1 teaspoon dry mustard
1 × 5 ml spoon curry powder	1 teaspoon curry powder
4 chicken joints	4 chicken joints
300 ml chicken stock	½ pint chicken stock
2 × 15 ml spoons concentrated tomato purée	2 tablespoons concentrated tomato purée
Salt and freshly ground black pepper	Salt and freshly ground black pepper
To finish:	To finish:
Parsley, finely chopped	Parsley, finely chopped

Cooking Time: 1 hour
Oven: 180°C, 350°F, Gas Mark 4

Heat the oil and sauté the onions and garlic until soft. Mix together the mustard and curry powder and rub into the chicken joints. Add these to the pan and sauté until golden. Mix together the stock and tomato purée, pour over the chicken, season to taste. Place in a casserole and bake in a moderate oven for 1 hour. Garnish with chopped parsley.
Calories per portion: 270 1,110 kJ

Chicken in tomato sauce

Metric	Imperial
4 chicken breasts	4 chicken breasts
1 × 5 ml spoon salt and pepper	1 teaspoon salt and pepper
Dash of paprika	Dash of paprika
396 g can tomatoes	14 oz can tomatoes
1 onion, peeled and thinly sliced into rings	1 onion, peeled and thinly sliced into rings
100 g mushrooms, cleaned	4 oz mushrooms, cleaned
2 × 15 ml spoons finely chopped parsley	2 tablespoons finely chopped parsley
½ teaspoon oregano	½ teaspoon oregano
½ teaspoon celery seed	½ teaspoon celery seed
1 clove garlic, chopped	1 clove garlic, chopped
1 bay leaf	1 bay leaf

Cooking Time: 1 hour 10 minutes
Oven: 180°C, 350°F, Gas Mark 4

Place the chicken breasts in a deep baking dish and sprinkle with salt, pepper and paprika. Drain the tomatoes, reserving 3 × 15 ml spoons (3 tablespoons) juice. Arrange tomatoes, onion and sliced mushrooms over the chicken. Sprinkle with parsley, oregano and celery seed. Mix the reserved liquid, garlic and bay leaf and pour over chicken. Cover and bake in a moderate oven for 1 hour. Uncover and bake for 10 minutes more. Remove bay leaf and spoon juices over the chicken.
Calories per portion: 190 800 kJ

Chicken paprika; Chicken in tomato sauce; Bengal chicken curry

Seville chicken

Metric	Imperial
2 × 15 ml spoons oil	2 tablespoons oil
4 chicken joints	4 chicken joints
2 large onions, peeled and sliced	2 large onions, peeled and sliced
2 cloves garlic, crushed	2 cloves garlic, crushed
396 g can tomatoes	14 oz can tomatoes
300 ml chicken stock	½ pint chicken stock
Bouquet garni	Bouquet garni
Salt and freshly ground black pepper	Salt and freshly ground black pepper
2 red peppers, deseeded and sliced	2 red peppers, deseeded and sliced
65 ml sherry	2½ fl oz sherry

To finish:
12 stuffed green olives, sliced

To finish:
12 stuffed green olives, sliced

Cooking Time: 40 minutes

Brush the chicken joints with a little of the oil and grill quickly to brown. Remove and keep hot. Put a little more of the oil in a non-stick pan and sauté the onions and garlic until soft. Add the tomatoes, stock and bouquet garni. Season well and add the browned chicken joints. Cover and simmer for 30 minutes until tender. Heat the remaining oil in another pan and gently sauté two-thirds of the peppers, reserving the remainder for garnish. Add to the chicken. Strain the chicken from the sauce and put in a heated serving dish. Remove the bouquet garni, put the sauce into a liquidiser and blend until smooth. Add the sherry to the purée and adjust seasoning. Stir in the olives and pour over the chicken. Garnish with remaining peppers.
Calories per portion: 280 1,100 kJ

Chicken tandoori

Metric	Imperial
4 boned chicken breasts, 75 g in weight	4 boned chicken breasts, 3 oz in weight
1 onion, finely chopped	1 onion, finely chopped
2 × 142 g cartons natural yogurt	2 × 5 oz cartons natural yogurt
½ teaspoon ground ginger	½ teaspoon ground ginger
½ teaspoon paprika	½ teaspoon paprika
½ × 15 ml spoon curry powder	½ tablespoon curry powder
2 × 15 ml spoons lemon juice	2 tablespoons lemon juice
Rind of ½ lemon, finely grated	Rind of ½ lemon, finely grated
1 × 5 ml spoon salt	1 teaspoon salt
1 clove garlic, crushed	1 clove garlic, crushed

Cooking Time: 1½ hours Oven: 160°C, 325°F, Gas Mark 3

Remove any skin from the chicken breasts, prick all over and place in a shallow dish. Mix all the remaining ingredients together and spoon evenly over the chicken. Cover the dish and refrigerate for 24 hours.
Remove the chicken breasts from the marinade and stand on a rack in a roasting tin spooning over any remaining tandoori marinade. Cook in a slow oven for 1½ hours. Serve with a crisp salad.
Calories per portion: 150 600 kJ

Cheese and sweetcorn soufflé

Metric

40 g butter
40 g plain flour
300 ml hot skimmed milk
4 × 15 ml spoons sweetcorn
purée
75 g Edam cheese, grated
Salt and freshly ground
black pepper
3 large eggs, separated

Imperial

1½ oz butter
1½ oz plain flour
½ pint hot skimmed milk
4 tablespoons sweetcorn
purée
3 oz Edam cheese, grated
Salt and freshly ground
black pepper
3 large eggs, separated

Cooking Time: 40–45 minutes
Oven: 190°C, 375°F, Gas Mark 5

Melt the butter in a heavy-based saucepan, stir in the flour and cook over a low heat for 3 minutes. Remove from the heat and add the hot milk, a little at a time. Bring to the boil and cook until smooth and thick. Add the sweetcorn purée and grated cheese and season to taste. Beat the egg yolks thoroughly and blend into the corn and cheese mixture. Beat the egg whites until very stiff and blend into the corn and cheese mixture. Pour into a prepared 1 l (2 pint) soufflé dish and bake in the centre of a moderately hot oven for 45 minutes until golden. Serve immediately.
Calories per portion: 260 1,050 kJ

Chicken and egg balls

Metric

6 hard-boiled eggs, shelled
3 × 15 ml spoons finely
chopped chives
250 g cooked chicken
5 × 15 ml spoons low-
calorie mayonnaise
Salt and freshly ground
black pepper
25 g low-calorie bread-
crumbs, browned
4 × 15 ml spoons finely
chopped parsley

To finish:
Lettuce
Tomato wedges
Parsley sprigs

Imperial

6 hard-boiled eggs, shelled
3 tablespoons finely
chopped chives
9 oz cooked chicken
5 tablespoons low-
calorie mayonnaise
Salt and freshly ground
black pepper
1 oz low-calorie bread-
crumbs, browned
4 tablespoons finely
chopped parsley

To finish:
Lettuce
Tomato wedges
Parsley sprigs

Dice the hard-boiled eggs and mix with the chopped chives. Mince the chicken and add, with the mayonnaise. Mix to bind and season to taste. Divide the mixture into 12 and roll each portion into a ball. Combine the breadcrumbs and chopped parsley and lightly roll each ball in this mixture to coat evenly. Chill thoroughly. Serve on a bed of lettuce garnished with the tomato wedges and sprigs of parsley.
Calories per portion: 290 1,200 kJ

Oeufs florentine

Metric

½ kg spinach
Salt and freshly ground
black pepper
25 g butter
25 g flour
300 ml skimmed milk
50 g Edam cheese, grated
4 eggs

To finish:
Tomato slices (optional)

Imperial

1 lb spinach
Salt and freshly ground
black pepper
1 oz butter
1 oz flour
½ pint skimmed milk
2 oz Edam cheese, grated
4 eggs

To finish:
Tomato slices (optional)

Cooking Time: 20–25 minutes

Wash the spinach well, trim and put into a pan with a little salt and just the water that clings to the leaves. Cook for 10–15 minutes until tender. Meanwhile make a cheese sauce by melting the butter, blending in the flour and cooking for 1 minute. Gradually stir in the milk and bring to the boil, stirring. Cook for 2 minutes and then stir in the grated cheese. Drain the spinach well, chop roughly and season generously. Put into an ovenproof dish. Poach the eggs lightly, drain, and place side by side on the spinach. Pour the sauce over the spinach and put under a hot grill until golden. Garnish with tomato slices if liked.
Calories per portion: 250 1,050 kJ

Chicken and egg balls; Cheese and sweetcorn soufflé; Oeufs florentine

Breakfast scramble; Baked eggs

Baked eggs

Metric	Imperial
25 g butter	1 oz butter
4 eggs	4 eggs
Salt and freshly ground	Salt and freshly ground
black pepper	black pepper
Parsley sprigs	Parsley sprigs

Cooking Time: 5–8 minutes
Oven: 180°C, 350°F, Gas Mark 4

Preheat the oven to moderate. Place 4 individual ovenproof ramekin dishes or cocottes on a baking sheet. Place a knob of butter in each. Put in the oven for 1–2 minutes until the butter has melted. Break an egg into each dish, sprinkle with a little salt and pepper and cook in the centre of the oven until the eggs are just set—5–8 minutes. Garnish with parsley and serve at once.
Calories per portion: 145 600 kJ

Breakfast scramble

Metric	Imperial
25 g butter	1 oz butter
3 green peppers, deseeded and chopped	3 green peppers, deseeded and chopped
4 eggs	4 eggs
75 ml skimmed milk	3 fl oz skimmed milk
50 g ham, chopped	2 oz ham, chopped
4 slices low-calorie bread, toasted	4 slices low-calorie bread, toasted
50 g Edam cheese, grated	2 oz Edam cheese, grated

Cooking Time: 5 minutes

Melt the butter in a non-stick pan and sauté the green pepper. Beat the eggs and milk, pour over the pepper and cook in the normal way. When almost cooked add the chopped ham. Serve on slices of low-calorie toast sprinkled with the grated cheese.
Calories per portion: 275 1,100 kJ

Cheese and fish scallops; Soufflé omelette

Soufflé omelette

Metric

2 eggs, separated
1 × 5 ml spoon water
Salt and freshly ground
black pepper
10 g butter

Imperial

2 eggs, separated
1 teaspoon water
Salt and freshly ground
black pepper
¼ oz butter

Preheat a grill to moderately hot, and gently heat an omelette pan. Whisk the egg whites until they stand in soft peaks. Whisk the egg yolks with the cold water until pale and creamy and season generously. Fold in the egg whites. Melt the butter in the omelette pan, pour in the egg mixture and level the top. Cook without moving until the bottom is set and golden—about 2–3 minutes. Place under the grill for about ½ minute. Fold in half, slide on to a warm plate and serve immediately. Serves 1.
Calories per portion: 210 815 kJ

Cheese and fish scallops

Metric

½ kg white fish fillets
Skimmed milk
25 g butter
25 g flour
300 ml skimmed milk
40 g Edam cheese, grated
Salt and freshly ground
black pepper
225 g mashed potato

To finish:
Parsley sprigs

Imperial

1 lb white fish fillets
Skimmed milk
1 oz butter
1 oz flour
½ pint skimmed milk
1½ oz Edam cheese, grated
Salt and freshly ground
black pepper
8 oz mashed potato

To finish:
Parsley sprigs

Cooking Time: 15–20 minutes

Poach the fish fillets in skimmed milk until cooked. Drain and flake. Melt the butter in a heavy-based saucepan, stir in the flour and cook for 2–3 minutes. Remove from heat and stir in the milk a little at a time. Bring to the boil and cook for 2–3 minutes until smooth and thick. Stir in the grated cheese and season to taste. Fold in the flaked fish, spoon into 4 scallop shells or small dishes. Pipe the cooked potato around this. Cook under a hot grill until golden and bubbly. Garnish with the parsley.
Calories per portion: 225 950 kJ

Spinach and egg niçoise

Metric	Imperial
225 g frozen spinach	8 oz frozen spinach
1 small red pepper, deseeded and chopped	1 small red pepper, deseeded and chopped
225 g tomatoes, peeled and chopped	8 oz tomatoes, peeled and chopped
15 g butter	½ oz butter
Salt and freshly ground black pepper	Salt and freshly ground black pepper
4 eggs	4 eggs

Cooking Time: 10–15 minutes

Cook the frozen spinach according to the directions on the packet. Meanwhile sauté the red pepper and tomatoes in the butter until soft. Place the spinach in the bottom of a shallow heatproof dish. Top with the tomato and pepper mixture and season to taste. Make four hollows in the mixture and break the eggs into them. Cook over a low heat until just set. Serve immediately.

Calories per portion: 160 650 kJ

Piperade

Metric	Imperial
1 × 15 ml spoon olive oil	1 tablespoon olive oil
1 large onion, peeled and finely chopped	1 large onion, peeled and finely chopped
2 green peppers, cored and cut into large strips	2 green peppers, cored and cut into large strips
1 clove garlic (optional)	1 clove garlic (optional)
½ kg tomatoes, peeled	1 lb tomatoes, peeled
4 eggs	4 eggs
4 gammon rashers, trimmed	4 gammon rashers, trimmed
Salt and freshly ground black pepper	Salt and freshly ground black pepper

Cooking Time: 30 minutes

Heat the oil in a large non-stick pan and cook the chopped onions until soft. Add the peppers and garlic and cook gently for about 5 minutes. Add the roughly chopped tomatoes and season to taste. Cover and cook for 20 minutes. Lightly beat the eggs, pour on to the cooked vegetables and stir until just set. Meanwhile grill the gammon rashers, timing the grilling so they are cooked when the eggs are just set. Serve on a warmed flat dish with the gammon rashers arranged on top.

Calories per portion: 430 1,750 kJ

Spicy rarebit

Metric	Imperial
225 g Edam cheese, grated	8 oz Edam cheese, grated
4 eggs, beaten	4 eggs, beaten
Few drops Worcestershire sauce	Few drops Worcestershire sauce
Salt and freshly ground black pepper	Salt and freshly ground black pepper
2 × 5 ml spoons flour	2 teaspoons flour
4 slices low-calorie bread	4 slices low-calorie bread
50 g cooked ham, diced	2 oz cooked ham, diced
Tomato slices	Tomato slices

Cooking Time: 5 minutes

Mix together the cheese and the beaten eggs, add a few drops of Worcestershire sauce and season to taste. Whisk in the flour. Toast the bread on one side. Place equal quantities of the egg mixture on the uncooked sides of the bread. Sprinkle with the diced ham and grill until golden. Serve hot with slices of tomato.

Calories per portion: 305 1,200 kJ

Egg mayonnaise

Metric	Imperial
4 eggs	4 eggs
1 lettuce	1 lettuce
½ cucumber, thinly sliced	½ cucumber, thinly sliced
4 tomatoes, quartered	4 tomatoes, quartered
8 × 15 ml spoons Slimmer's Mayonnaise (page 69)	8 tablespoons Slimmer's Mayonnaise (page 69)
To finish:	To finish:
1 bunch watercress, washed and trimmed	1 bunch watercress, washed and trimmed

Hard-boil the eggs, shell and halve. Wash and dry the lettuce and use to line four individual plates. Place the eggs cut side down on the lettuce and arrange the cucumber and tomatoes decoratively around them. Spoon the mayonnaise over the eggs and garnish with the watercress. Chill before serving.

Calories per portion: 135 550 kJ

Spinach and egg niçoise; Spicy rarebit; Egg mayonnaise; Piperade; Herby cheese omelette

Herby cheese omelette

Metric

2 eggs, separated
1 × 15 ml spoon water
1 × 5 ml spoon mixed herbs
Salt and freshly ground
black pepper
25 g Edam cheese, grated

Imperial

2 eggs, separated
1 tablespoon water
1 teaspoon mixed herbs
Salt and freshly ground
black pepper
1 oz Edam cheese, grated

Cooking Time: about 10 minutes

Beat the egg yolks with the water, herbs and seasoning to taste. Whisk the egg whites until stiff and fold into the egg yolk mixture. Pour into a preheated non-stick pan and cook gently over a moderate heat, disturbing the mixture occasionally, until the underneath is set. Sprinkle with the grated cheese and place under a preheated high grill until the top puffs and turns golden.
Serves 1.
Calories per portion: 250 750 kJ

Artichoke and cottage cheese salad

Mixed spring salad with herb dressing

Metric

3 × 15 ml spoons finely chopped mixed fresh herbs
6 × 15 ml spoons Slimmer's French Dressing (page 71)
1 clove garlic, crushed
Salt and freshly ground black pepper
1 lettuce, washed
1 bunch of watercress, cleaned and trimmed
4 spring onions, washed and diced

To finish:
Spring onions, cleaned and trimmed

Imperial

3 tablespoons finely chopped mixed fresh herbs
6 tablespoons Slimmer's French Dressing (page 71)
1 clove garlic, crushed
Salt and freshly ground black pepper
1 lettuce, washed
1 bunch of watercress, cleaned and trimmed
4 spring onions, washed and diced

To finish:
Spring onions, cleaned and trimmed

Mix together the herbs, dressing, garlic and seasoning to taste. Leave to stand for 2 hours. In a large bowl mix together the shredded lettuce, watercress and spring onions. Pour over the dressing and serve garnished with the whole spring onions.
Calories per portion: 75 300 kJ

Orange and mint salad

Metric

4 large oranges
2 × 15 ml spoons finely chopped mint
4 × 15 ml spoons lemon juice
6 × 15 ml spoons wine vinegar
Liquid sweetener
Salt and freshly ground black pepper

To finish:
Mint sprigs

Imperial

4 large oranges
2 tablespoons finely chopped mint
4 tablespoons lemon juice
6 tablespoons wine vinegar
Liquid sweetener
Salt and freshly ground black pepper

To finish:
Mint sprigs

Remove all the peel and pith from the oranges and cut the flesh into thin slices. Place in a serving dish and sprinkle with the chopped mint. Mix the lemon juice with the vinegar, adding sweetener to taste. Season with salt and pepper and pour over the orange and mint. Garnish with sprigs of mint.
Calories per portion: 52 200 kJ

Artichoke and cottage cheese salad

Metric

350 g cottage cheese
1 small onion, finely grated
Salt and freshly ground
black pepper
396 g can artichoke
hearts
4 × 15 ml spoons natural
yogurt
4 × 15 ml spoons lemon
juice
2 × 15 ml spoons finely
chopped parsley

To finish:
4 lemon slices

Imperial

12 oz cottage cheese
1 small onion, finely grated
Salt and freshly ground
black pepper
14 oz can artichoke
hearts
4 tablespoons natural
yogurt
4 tablespoons lemon
juice
2 tablespoons finely
chopped parsley

To finish:
4 lemon slices

Mix the cottage cheese with the grated onion and season to taste. Divide between four individual serving dishes and pile into the centre of each. Drain the artichoke hearts and cut them into quarters. Arrange around the mounds of cottage cheese. Mix the yogurt with the lemon juice and parsley, season to taste and spoon over the cottage cheese. Garnish each dish with a twist of lemon.
Calories per portion: 120 500 kJ

Mixed spring salad with herb dressing; Orange and mint salad

Cucumber and fennel salad

Metric	Imperial
1 large cucumber	1 large cucumber
75 g fennel	3 oz fennel
2 × 15 ml spoons finely chopped parsley	2 tablespoons finely chopped parsley
1 small onion, finely sliced	1 small onion, finely sliced
1 box mustard and cress	1 box mustard and cress
4 × 15 ml spoons Slimmer's French Dressing (page 71)	4 tablespoons Slimmer's French Dressing (page 71)

Wash and finely slice the unpeeled cucumber and place in a salad bowl. Wash and grate the fennel and add to the cucumber with all the remaining ingredients. Toss lightly and serve.

Calories per portion: 18 80 kJ

Peach and soured cream salad

Metric	Imperial
1 lettuce, washed and shredded	1 lettuce, washed and shredded
4 medium firm peaches	4 medium firm peaches
2 × 5 ml spoons mild curry powder	2 teaspoons mild curry powder
1 drop liquid sweetener	1 drop liquid sweetener
2 × 15 ml spoons lemon juice	2 tablespoons lemon juice
4 × 15 ml spoons soured cream	4 tablespoons soured cream
1 clove of garlic, very finely chopped	1 clove of garlic, very finely chopped

Arrange the shredded lettuce on four individual plates. Wash and stone the peaches, then slice into 1.5 cm ($\frac{1}{2}$ in) pieces. Mix together the curry powder, sweetener, lemon juice, soured cream and garlic. Arrange the peaches on top of the lettuce and spoon over the soured cream dressing. Chill before using.

Calories per portion: 68 300 kJ

Bacon and radish salad

Metric	Imperial
4 rashers lean bacon	4 rashers lean bacon
4 sticks of celery, scrubbed	4 sticks of celery, scrubbed
24 large radishes	24 large radishes
3 × 15 ml spoons Slimmer's French Dressing (page 71)	3 tablespoons Slimmer's French Dressing (page 71)
2 × 5 ml spoons finely chopped fresh sage	2 teaspoons finely chopped fresh sage
To finish: Watercress sprig	To finish: Watercress sprig

Grill the bacon until crisp, drain on absorbent paper and chop into small pieces. Slice the celery and radishes. Mix the dressing with the chopped sage, add to the bacon, celery and radishes. Toss lightly to coat and serve at once garnished with a sprig of watercress.

Calories per portion: 87 300 kJ

Sunkissed salad

Metric	Imperial
$\frac{1}{2}$ kg French beans, washed and trimmed	1 lb French beans, washed and trimmed
$\frac{1}{2}$ kg cottage cheese	1 lb cottage cheese
6 eggs, hard-boiled	6 eggs, hard-boiled
2 red peppers, deseeded and sliced	2 red peppers, deseeded and sliced
4 × 15 ml spoons Slimmer's French Dressing (page 71)	4 tablespoons Slimmer's French Dressing (page 71)

Cooking Time: 10–15 minutes

Cook the beans in boiling salted water until tender—about 10–15 minutes. Cool, then place on a large round serving dish. Pile the cottage cheese in the centre and surround with the quartered hard-boiled eggs. Garnish with the chopped red pepper, between the eggs and around the cottage cheese. Just before serving pour the dressing over the beans and pepper slices.

Calories per portion: 295 1,200 kJ

Bacon and radish salad; Cucumber and fennel salad; Peach and soured cream salad; Sunkissed salad

Tomato juice dressing

Metric

300 ml tomato juice
1 × 15 ml spoon tarragon
vinegar
1 clove garlic, crushed
(optional)
Salt and freshly ground
black pepper

Imperial

½ pint tomato juice
1 tablespoon tarragon
vinegar
1 clove garlic, crushed
(optional)
Salt and freshly ground
black pepper

In a screw-topped jar shake together the tomato juice,
tarragon vinegar and garlic if used. Season to taste with salt
and pepper. Chill before use.
Calories per portion: 15 50 kJ

Apple and cabbage slaw

Metric

1 medium head of white
cabbage, washed
4 red apples, washed
1 × 15 ml spoon lemon juice
1 small green pepper,
washed and deseeded
1 medium onion, peeled
and finely sliced
6 × 15 ml spoons Slimmer's
French Dressing (page 71)
25 g Edam cheese, grated

Imperial

1 medium head of white
cabbage, washed
4 red apples, washed
1 tablespoon lemon juice
1 small green pepper,
washed and deseeded
1 medium onion, peeled
and finely sliced
6 tablespoons Slimmer's
French Dressing (page 71)
1 oz Edam cheese, grated

Shred the cabbage finely and place in a large bowl. Remove
the cores from the apples and slice apples thinly, sprinkling
with lemon juice to prevent them from going brown. Add
to the bowl with the diced green pepper, onion and dressing.
Toss lightly. Sprinkle with the grated cheese.
Serves 6.
Calories per portion: 112 450 kJ

Apple and cabbage slaw

Slimmer's mayonnaise

Metric	Imperial
1 × 15 ml rounded spoon cornflour	*1 rounded tablespoon cornflour*
1 × 5 ml spoon celery seed	*1 teaspoon celery seed*
1 × 5 ml spoon dry mustard	*1 teaspoon dry mustard*
1 × 5 ml spoon salt	*1 teaspoon salt*
250 ml skimmed milk	*8 fl oz skimmed milk*
2 egg yolks, beaten	*2 egg yolks, beaten*
50 ml vinegar	*2 fl oz vinegar*
2 drops liquid sweetener	*2 drops liquid sweetener*

Cooking Time: 10 minutes

Mix together the cornflour, celery seed, mustard and salt in a small heavy-based saucepan. Add the skimmed milk a little at a time and cook over a low heat, stirring constantly, until the mixture thickens. Continue to cook for 2 minutes. Cool slightly, add the beaten egg yolks and cook for a further 2–3 minutes. Remove from the heat and stir in the vinegar and sweetener. Chill before serving.
Makes 300 ml ($\frac{1}{2}$ pint).
Calories per 15 ml spoon (1 tablespoon): 15 50 kJ

Tomato juice dressing; Slimmer's mayonnaise

Salad niçoise

Metric

198 g can tuna fish
1 lettuce
65 g can anchovy
fillets, drained
2 hard-boiled eggs
4 tomatoes, quartered
2 sticks celery, scrubbed
1 small green pepper,
deseeded and chopped
1 small onion, peeled and
sliced into rings
Salt and freshly ground
black pepper
8 × 15 ml spoons Slimmer's
French Dressing (page 71)
12 black olives, stoned

Imperial

7 oz can tuna fish
1 lettuce
2½ oz can anchovy
fillets, drained
2 hard-boiled eggs
4 tomatoes, quartered
2 sticks celery, scrubbed
1 small green pepper,
deseeded and chopped
1 small onion, peeled and
sliced into rings
Salt and freshly ground
black pepper
8 tablespoons Slimmer's
French Dressing (page 71)
12 black olives, stoned

Drain the oil from the tuna fish and flake well. Wash and dry the lettuce. Shred and divide between four individual serving dishes. Mix the tuna with the anchovy fillets, eggs cut into 4–6 segments, tomatoes, half the chopped celery, pepper and onion rings, seasoning to taste and the dressing. Divide between the dishes and pile on top of the lettuce. Garnish with the remaining celery, pepper and onion rings and the black olives.

Calories per portion: 210 850 kJ

Salad niçoise; Hot cucumber salad

Hot cucumber salad

Metric

3 × 15 ml spoons Slimmer's
French Dressing (page 71)
1 small cucumber, thinly
sliced but not peeled
1 clove garlic, finely
chopped
1 large Cos lettuce heart,
washed and shredded
1 × 15 ml spoon fresh,
finely chopped dill
2 × 15 ml spoons lemon
juice
Salt and freshly ground
black pepper
To finish:
1 × 15 ml spoon finely
chopped parsley

Imperial

3 tablespoons Slimmer's
French Dressing (page 71)
1 small cucumber, thinly
sliced but not peeled
1 clove garlic, finely
chopped
1 large Cos lettuce heart,
washed and shredded
1 tablespoon fresh,
finely chopped dill
2 tablespoons lemon
juice
Salt and freshly ground
black pepper
To finish:
1 tablespoon finely
chopped parsley

Cooking Time: 5–10 minutes

Put the dressing in a pan on a moderate heat and cook the cucumber and garlic in it until the cucumber is just beginning to soften. Quickly stir in the lettuce, dill and lemon juice. Season to taste and serve immediately, garnished with the chopped parsley. Ideal to accompany grilled steak or chops.

Calories per portion: 42 150 kJ

Yogurt dressing; Slimmer's French dressing

Yogurt dressing

Metric

142 g carton natural yogurt
2 drops liquid sweetener
3 × 5 ml spoons lemon juice
2 × 5 ml spoons French mustard
1 × 5 ml spoon mixed dried herbs
3 × 15 ml spoons gherkins, finely chopped
Salt and freshly ground black pepper

Imperial

5 oz carton natural yogurt
2 drops liquid sweetener
3 teaspoons lemon juice
2 teaspoons French mustard
1 teaspoon mixed dried herbs
3 tablespoons gherkins, finely chopped
Salt and freshly ground black pepper

In a small bowl mix together the yogurt, sweetener, lemon juice, mustard and dried herbs. Add the finely chopped gherkins and season to taste. Chill before using.
Calories per portion: 20 80 kJ

Slimmer's French dressing

Metric

250 ml tomato juice
¼ teaspoon celery salt
1 × 5 ml spoon lemon juice
1 × 5 ml spoon onion, very finely chopped
¼ teaspoon Worcestershire sauce
¼ teaspoon prepared horseradish
1 clove garlic, crushed (optional)
Salt and freshly ground black pepper
Chopped shallot to garnish

Imperial

8 fl oz tomato juice
¼ teaspoon celery salt
1 teaspoon lemon juice
1 teaspoon onion, very finely chopped
¼ teaspoon Worcestershire sauce
¼ teaspoon prepared horseradish
1 clove garlic, crushed (optional)
Salt and freshly ground black pepper
Chopped shallot to garnish

Place all the ingredients together in a small screw-topped jar, cover and shake well. Use or store in the refrigerator.

Grilled courgettes with mustard

Metric	Imperial
½ kg courgettes, scrubbed and cut in half lengthwise	1 lb courgettes, scrubbed and cut in half lengthwise
25 g butter, melted	1 oz butter, melted
1 × 15 ml spoon Meaux mustard	1 tablespoon Meaux mustard

Cooking Time: about 10 minutes

Brush the courgettes with the melted butter and place them, cut side down, on a heated grill pan. Grill under a high heat until they are lightly brown. Turn them over and spread with the mustard. Return to the grill and cook until golden. Serve with roast or grilled meat.

Calories per portion: 67 300 kJ

Lemon glazed carrots

Metric	Imperial
1 bunch new carrots	1 bunch new carrots
15 g butter	½ oz butter
1 × 5 ml spoon soft brown sugar	1 teaspoon soft brown sugar
300 ml stock	½ pint stock
1 × 15 ml spoon finely chopped mint	1 tablespoon finely chopped mint
1 × 15 ml spoon lemon juice	1 tablespoon lemon juice
Salt and freshly ground black pepper	Salt and freshly ground black pepper

Cooking Time: 10–15 minutes

Scrub and trim the carrots and put into a pan with the butter and sugar. Barely cover with the stock. Bring to the boil and cook, uncovered, on a moderate heat until all the liquid has been absorbed and the carrots are glazed. Stir in the mint and the lemon juice, season if liked, and simmer for a further two minutes.

Calories per portion: 60 250 kJ

Celery au gratin

Metric	Imperial
1 head celery, scrubbed and chopped	1 head celery, scrubbed and chopped
Salt and freshly ground black pepper	Salt and freshly ground black pepper
25 g butter	1 oz butter
25 g flour	1 oz flour
150 ml skimmed milk	¼ pint skimmed milk
50 g Edam cheese, grated	2 oz Edam cheese, grated

Cooking Time: 25–30 minutes
Oven: 190°C, 375°F, Gas Mark 5

Cook the celery in a little boiling salted water for 10–15 minutes. Drain well, retaining 150 ml (¼ pint) of the liquor. Melt the butter in a small pan, blend in the flour and cook for 1 minute. Gradually add the celery liquor and the skimmed milk, stirring continuously until smooth. Add half the cheese and stir to blend. Fill an ovenproof dish with alternate layers of celery and sauce. Sprinkle with the remaining cheese and bake in a hot oven until lightly browned.

Calories per portion: 150 600 kJ

Grilled leeks

Metric	Imperial
675 g leeks, scrubbed and cut into 4 cm lengths	1½ lb leeks, scrubbed and cut into 1½ in lengths
25 g butter, softened	1 oz butter, softened
1 × 15 ml spoon grated Parmesan cheese	1 tablespoon grated Parmesan cheese
2 × 5 ml spoons Dijon mustard	2 teaspoons Dijon mustard

Cooking Time: 10–15 minutes

Cook the leeks in boiling salted water for about 10 minutes. Drain and transfer to a shallow heatproof dish. Cream together the butter, cheese and mustard and spread the mixture over the leeks. Cook under a hot grill until golden.

Calories per portion: 141 550 kJ

Grilled leeks; Lemon glazed carrots; Grilled courgettes with mustard; Celery au gratin

Red cabbage with caraway seeds and allspice; Fennel provençale style

Red cabbage with caraway seeds and allspice

Metric

1 medium red cabbage,
trimmed and cut into
wedges
1 × 15 ml spoon vinegar
2 × 5 ml spoons caraway
seeds
¼ teaspoon allspice
2 × 15 ml spoons soured
cream

Imperial

1 medium red cabbage,
trimmed and cut into
wedges
1 tablespoon vinegar
2 teaspoons caraway
seeds
¼ teaspoon allspice
2 tablespoons soured
cream

Cooking Time: 8–12 minutes

Wash the cabbage and place in a pan with 1.5 cm (½ in) of boiling salted water. Add the vinegar, caraway seeds and allspice. Cover with a tight-fitting lid and cook briskly for 8–12 minutes or until tender, shaking occasionally. Drain and serve with the soured cream.
Calories per portion: 44 150 kJ

Fennel provençale style

Metric

3 stalks (½ kg) fennel
50 g butter
150 ml stock
1 small onion, peeled and
finely chopped
½ clove garlic, crushed
396 g can tomatoes
Salt and freshly ground
black pepper

Imperial

3 stalks (1 lb) fennel
2 oz butter
¼ pint stock
1 small onion, peeled and
finely chopped
½ clove garlic, crushed
14 oz can tomatoes
Salt and freshly ground
black pepper

Cooking Time: 30–40 minutes

Separate the fennel stalks into ribs, wash thoroughly and discard any that are tough. Cut the ribs into 2.5 cm (1 in) lengths, cover with boiling water and leave to stand for 5 minutes. Drain well. Melt half the butter in a heavy-based pan, add the fennel and the stock. Cook very slowly for 30 minutes or until fennel is tender. Sauté the onion and garlic in the remaining butter and add to the fennel along with the tomatoes and seasoning to taste. Cover and cook for 10 more minutes. Serve hot.
Calories per portion: 130 572 kJ

Leeks in slimmer's celery and cheese sauce; Honey glazed peas and carrots

Honey glazed peas and carrots

Metric

½ kg peas, shelled
225 g new baby carrots
1 × 15 ml spoon finely
chopped mint
25 g butter
450 ml stock
2 × 5 ml spoons honey
Salt and freshly ground
black pepper

Imperial

1 lb peas, shelled
8 oz new baby carrots
1 tablespoon finely
chopped mint
1 oz butter
¾ pint stock
2 teaspoons honey
Salt and freshly ground
black pepper

Cooking Time: 10–15 minutes

Put the peas and carrots in a saucepan with the mint and butter and just cover with the stock. Add the honey and boil briskly, uncovered, until all the stock is absorbed and the vegetables are glazed—about 10–15 minutes. Season to taste before serving.

Calories per portion: 120 500 kJ

Leeks in slimmer's celery and cheese sauce

Metric

½ kg leeks, washed and
cut into 4 cm lengths
524 g can celery hearts
2 × 15 ml spoons dried
skimmed milk
50 g Cheddar cheese,
grated
Freshly ground black
pepper

Imperial

1 lb leeks, washed and
cut into 1½ in lengths
1 lb 2½ oz can celery hearts
2 tablespoons dried
skimmed milk
2 oz Cheddar cheese,
grated
Freshly ground black
pepper

Cooking Time: about 15 minutes

Cook the leeks in boiling salted water for about 10 minutes until tender. Meanwhile sieve or purée the contents of the can of celery hearts and whisk in the dried milk. Bring to the boil, stirring, then remove from heat. Add two-thirds of the cheese and pepper to taste, blending thoroughly. Drain the leeks and place in a shallow heat-proof dish, pour over the sauce and sprinkle with the remaining cheese. Put under a hot grill until golden.

Calories per portion: 132 550 kJ

Sauerkraut

Metric	*Imperial*
1 red cabbage, washed and finely shredded	*1 red cabbage, washed and finely shredded*
Handful of cooking salt	*Handful of cooking salt*
2 × 15 ml spoons lemon juice	*2 tablespoons lemon juice*
1 large onion, finely chopped	*1 large onion, finely chopped*
1 × 15 ml spoon olive oil	*1 tablespoon olive oil*
12 peppercorns	*12 peppercorns*
1 bay leaf	*1 bay leaf*
1 × 5 ml spoon caraway seeds	*1 teaspoon caraway seeds*
Rind of ½ lemon, grated	*Rind of ½ lemon, grated*
2 × 15 ml spoons vinegar	*2 tablespoons vinegar*
1–2 drops sweetener	*1–2 drops sweetener*
250 ml white stock	*8 fl oz white stock*

Cooking Time: about 15 minutes

Place the cabbage in a large bowl and sprinkle over the salt and the lemon juice. Mix well together then cover with a small plate and weight it down to press the cabbage. Leave for 1 hour, then squeeze the cabbage with your hands to remove excess juice and until the cabbage has reduced to half its original bulk. Wash under running cold water and squeeze again.

Sauté the chopped onion in the olive oil until golden. Add the cabbage and cook for 10 minutes. Add the peppercorns, bay leaf, caraway seeds, lemon rind, vinegar, sweetener and stock. Sauté together until the cabbage is tender, adding more stock if necessary. Serve hot with roast poultry or grills; or cool and serve as a salad.

Calories per portion: 75 300 kJ

Cauliflower Italiano

Metric	*Imperial*
2 × 15 ml spoons Slimmer's French dressing (page 71)	*2 tablespoons Slimmer's French dressing (page 71)*
1 × 15 ml spoon onion, finely chopped	*1 tablespoon onion, finely chopped*
1 clove garlic, crushed	*1 clove garlic, crushed*
1 medium cauliflower, washed and broken into florets	*1 medium cauliflower, washed and broken into florets*
2 × 15 ml spoons finely chopped green pepper	*2 tablespoons finely chopped green pepper*
	6 small tomatoes, peeled
Pinch of salt	*Pinch of salt*
Pinch of dried basil	*Pinch of dried basil*

Cooking Time: about 20 minutes

Pour the salad dressing into a deep frying pan and cook the onion and garlic in it until tender. Add the cauliflower with 3 × 15 ml spoons (3 tablespoons) water. Cook, covered, over a low heat for about 10 minutes. Add the chopped pepper and cook for a further 5 minutes. Stir in the remaining ingredients, heat through, check seasoning and serve.

Calories per portion: 54 200 kJ

Baked stuffed aubergines

Metric	*Imperial*
2 aubergines, washed	*2 aubergines, washed*
50 g low-calorie breadcrumbs	*2 oz low-calorie breadcrumbs*
1 onion, peeled	*1 onion, peeled*
50 g mushrooms, cleaned	*2 oz mushrooms, cleaned*
25 g butter	*1 oz butter*
1 egg, beaten	*1 egg, beaten*
50 g Edam cheese, grated	*2 oz Edam cheese, grated*
1 × 15 ml spoon finely chopped parsley	*1 tablespoon finely chopped parsley*
Salt and freshly ground black pepper	*Salt and freshly ground black pepper*
Skimmed milk	*Skimmed milk*

Cooking Time: 45 minutes
Oven: 180°C, 350°F, Gas Mark 4

Cut each aubergine in half lengthways, scoop out some of the inner flesh and place the cases in a shallow ovenproof casserole. Chop the aubergine flesh and mix with the breadcrumbs. Chop the onion and mushrooms and sauté in the butter until soft. Add the aubergine and breadcrumbs, together with the beaten egg, half the cheese, parsley and seasoning to taste. Moisten with a little skimmed milk if necessary. Fill the cases with this mixture, sprinkle with the remaining cheese and bake in a moderate oven for 35–45 minutes.

Calories per portion: 175 700 kJ

Baked stuffed aubergines; Cauliflower Italiano; Sauerkraut

Baked stuffed apples; Strawberry soufflé

Baked stuffed apples

Metric

4 medium cooking apples
150 ml dry cider
Liquid sweetener
100 g grapes, washed,
halved and depipped
4 small bunches of grapes,
washed
Little egg white
25 g desiccated coconut

Imperial

4 medium cooking apples
¼ pint dry cider
Liquid sweetener
4 oz grapes, washed,
halved and depipped
4 small bunches of grapes,
washed
Little egg white
1 oz desiccated coconut

Cooking Time: 45 minutes
Oven: 180°C, 350°F, Gas Mark 4

Wash and core the apples and put into a shallow ovenproof dish. Mix the cider with sweetener—allow for the tartness of the apples. Pack the grapes into the centre of each apple and pour over the cider mixture. Cover with foil and bake in a preheated moderate oven for 45 minutes. Meanwhile dip each small bunch of grapes in a little egg white and roll in the coconut. Allow to dry. Garnish each baked apple with a bunch of the frosted grapes.
Calories per portion: 112 450 kJ

Strawberry soufflé

Metric

½ kg fresh strawberries
25 g powdered gelatine
400 ml boiling water
600 ml low-calorie orange
squash, undiluted
2 × 5 ml spoons finely
grated lemon rind
Cold water
Liquid sweetener

Imperial

1 lb fresh strawberries
1 oz powdered gelatine
14 fl oz boiling water
1 pint low-calorie orange
squash, undiluted
2 teaspoons finely
grated lemon rind
Cold water
Liquid sweetener

Purée half the strawberries in a blender or push through a fine sieve. Dissolve the gelatine in the hot water, then stir in the squash and lemon rind. Make up to 1.2 l (2 pints) with cold water. Sweeten to taste with the liquid sweetener. Leave to chill until just beginning to set. Whisk until light and foamy, fold in the strawberry purée and spoon into shallow dessert dishes. Chill until firm and set. Just before serving top with the remaining hulled and sliced strawberries.
Calories per portion: 50 200 kJ

Rhubarb fool; Orange pots

Orange pots

Metric	Imperial
3 × 15 ml spoons orange juice	3 tablespoons orange juice
4 × 5 ml spoons lemon juice	4 teaspoons lemon juice
4 × 5 ml spoons powdered gelatine	4 teaspoons powdered gelatine
350 g cottage cheese	12 oz cottage cheese
6 × 15 ml spoons buttermilk	6 tablespoons buttermilk
Liquid sweetener	Liquid sweetener

To finish:
1 orange, thinly sliced

To finish:
1 orange, thinly sliced

Cooking Time: 5 minutes

Put the orange and lemon juice in a small bowl and sprinkle the gelatine over the top. Stand over a bowl of hot, but not boiling, water to dissolve the gelatine. Put the orange gelatine into a blender with the cottage cheese and buttermilk and blend until smooth. Add liquid sweetener to taste. Divide the mixture between four dessert glasses and decorate with quartered slices of orange.
Calories per portion: 135 550 kJ

Rhubarb fool

Metric	Imperial
½ kg rhubarb	1 lb rhubarb
2 × 15 ml spoons lemon juice	2 tablespoons lemon juice
Rind of ½ lemon, finely grated	Rind of ½ lemon, finely grated
Liquid sweetener	Liquid sweetener
2 egg yolks	2 egg yolks
142 g carton natural yogurt	5 oz carton natural yogurt

Cooking Time: 10 minutes

Wash and trim the rhubarb. Cut into 5 cm (2 in) lengths. Put into a saucepan with the lemon juice, grated lemon rind and sweetener to taste. Add 3 × 15 ml spoons (3 tablespoons) water and simmer gently until tender. Blend in a liquidiser or sieve. When cool beat in the egg yolks and fold in the yogurt so that the fool is streaked with threads of rhubarb. Spoon into sundae dishes and chill.
Calories per portion: 54 200 kJ

Ginger fruit salad

Metric

2 apples, washed and cored
but not peeled
2 apricots, peeled
1 orange, peeled
241 ml bottle low-
calorie ginger ale
2 bananas
2 × 15 ml spoons lemon
juice
50 g green grapes, washed
and depipped

Imperial

2 apples, washed and cored
but not peeled
2 apricots, peeled
1 orange, peeled
8½ fl oz bottle low-
calorie ginger ale
2 bananas
2 tablespoons lemon
juice
2 oz green grapes, washed
and depipped

Dice the apples and apricots, remove pith from the orange and divide into segments. Mix together in a bowl and pour over the ginger ale. Slice the bananas and mix with the lemon juice and grapes. Mix all fruit and juices together and serve in individual glasses.
Calories per portion: 70 300 kJ

Orange sorbet

Metric

2 × 15 ml spoons lemon
juice
1 × 5 ml spoon liquid
sweetener
Grated rind of 1 orange
170 g can unsweetened
concentrated orange juice
1 egg white
Orange slices

Imperial

2 tablespoons lemon
juice
1 teaspoon liquid
sweetener
Grated rind of 1 orange
6 oz can unsweetened
concentrated orange juice
1 egg white
Orange slices

Mix together the lemon juice and sweetener and make up to 300 ml (½ pint) with water. Add the orange rind and orange juice and pour into an ice cube tray. Freeze until just firm. Turn out into a mixing bowl and mash with a fork until the crystals are broken down. Whisk the egg white until stiff and fold into the mixture with a metal spoon. Return to the ice tray and freeze until firm. Soften slightly in the refrigerator for about 20 minutes before serving. Finish with twists of orange.
Calories per portion: 100 400 kJ

Orange sorbet; Ginger fruit salad

Grape jelly

Metric

15 g powdered gelatine
150 ml boiling water
450 ml unsweetened grape juice
Green colouring
225 g green grapes, washed and peeled
225 g cottage cheese
2 × 142 g cartons natural yogurt

Imperial

½ oz powdered gelatine
¼ pint boiling water
¾ pint unsweetened grape juice
Green colouring
½ lb green grapes, washed and peeled
8 oz cottage cheese
2 × 5 oz cartons natural yogurt

Dissolve the gelatine in the hot water and add the grape juice, with a few drops of colouring. Pour into 6 tall glasses. Divide the grapes between the glasses and leave tilted in a cool place to set. Blend or sieve the cottage cheese until smooth. Fold in the yogurt and top up the glasses. Chill before serving.
Serves 6.
Calories per portion: 110 450 kJ

Grape jelly

Lemon and blackcurrant fluff

Metric	Imperial
Half a 141 g tablet lemon-flavoured jelly	Half a 5 oz tablet lemon-flavoured jelly
65 ml boiling water	2½ fl oz boiling water
¼ teaspoon finely grated lemon rind	¼ teaspoon finely grated lemon rind
1 × 15 ml spoon lemon juice	1 tablespoon lemon juice
1 egg white	1 egg white
100 g fresh blackcurrants	4 oz fresh blackcurrants
1½ × 5 ml spoons cornflour	1½ teaspoons cornflour
2 × 15 ml spoons cold water	2 tablespoons cold water
Few drops of vanilla essence	Few drops of vanilla essence
Liquid sweetener	Liquid sweetener

Dissolve the lemon jelly in a large bowl with the boiling water. Make up to 250 ml (8 fl oz) with cold water. Stir in the lemon rind and juice. Chill until almost set. Add the egg white to the jelly mixture and beat with an electric whisk until light and fluffy—about 2 minutes. Pour into a mould or 4 ramekin dishes and chill until firm.

Meanwhile crush a third of the blackcurrants in a saucepan. Blend together the cornflour and cold water and add to the crushed blackcurrants. Cook over a medium heat, stirring constantly, until the mixture is thick and bubbly. Remove from heat and stir in remaining blackcurrants and vanilla essence. Sweeten to taste. To serve unmould the lemon fluff into a dish and spoon over the sauce.

Calories per portion: 60 300 kJ

Passion fruit pavlova

Metric	Imperial
3 large egg whites	3 large egg whites
1 × 5 ml spoon cream of tartar	1 teaspoon cream of tartar
3 × 15 ml spoons dry skimmed milk	3 tablespoons dry skimmed milk
6 saccharin tablets, crushed	6 saccharin tablets, crushed
4 passion fruit	4 passion fruit
2 oranges, peeled and segmented	2 oranges, peeled and segmented
To finish:	To finish:
Mint sprigs	Mint sprigs

Cooking Time: 30 minutes
Oven: 150°C, 300°F, Gas Mark 2

Whisk the egg whites lightly, sprinkle in the cream of tartar and continue whisking until the mixture forms peaks. Fold in the skimmed milk and crushed saccharin tablets, a tablespoon at a time, until the peaks are stiff. Draw a circle round a 20 cm (8 in) plate on a piece of non-stick paper. Place on a baking sheet and spread the meringue smoothly in the circle. Cook in a cool oven for about ½ hour. Cool, loosen carefully with a palette knife and lift on to a serving dish. Scoop out the centres of the passion fruit and pile on top of the meringue, alternating with orange segments. Garnish with sprigs of mint.

Calories per portion: 90 350 kJ

Apple mousse

Metric	Imperial
½ kg cooking apples, cleaned, cored and sliced	1 lb cooking apples, cleaned, cored and sliced
3 × 15 ml spoons water	3 tablespoons water
300 ml unsweetened grapefruit juice	½ pint unsweetened grapefruit juice
3 × 5 ml spoons gelatine	3 teaspoons gelatine
Few drops of liquid sweetener	Few drops of liquid sweetener
1 egg white	1 egg white
1–2 drops of green food colouring (optional)	1–2 drops of green food colouring (optional)
Pinch of nutmeg	Pinch of nutmeg

Simmer the apples with the water until tender (reserving a few slices for garnish). Heat a little of the grapefruit juice and dissolve the gelatine in it. When the apple has cooled slightly sieve or liquidise with the dissolved gelatine. Whisk in the remaining grapefruit juice with sweetener to taste. Place the mixture in an ice tray and freeze until beginning to set.

Whisk the egg white until stiff. Take out the apple purée and whisk again until frothy, adding the colouring and nutmeg. Fold in the egg white and freeze until stiff but not solid. Spoon into individual serving dishes and top with slices of apple.

Calories per portion: 94 400 kJ

Apple mousse; Passion fruit pavlova; Lemon and blackcurrant fluff

Orange and lemon cooler

Metric	Imperial
4 × 241 ml bottles low-calorie bitter lemon	4 × 8½ fl oz bottles low-calorie bitter lemon
1 × 170 g can frozen orange juice concentrate, thawed	1 × 6 oz can frozen orange juice concentrate, thawed

To finish:
Lemon slices
Mint sprigs

To finish:
Lemon slices
Mint sprigs

Pour the bitter lemon drink into ice trays and freeze until firm. Break into cubes and crush with a rolling pin or in a liquidiser. Pour the orange juice into a liquidiser and add the bitter lemon ice a little at a time, blending to mix well. Spoon into glasses and top with a twist of lemon and a sprig of mint.
Calories per portion: 60 250 kJ

Green summer cooler

Metric	Imperial
4 × 5 ml spoons crème de menthe	4 teaspoons crème de menthe
Crushed ice	Crushed ice
600 ml dry white wine	1 pint dry white wine
Perrier water	Perrier water

To finish:
Mint sprigs (optional)

To finish:
Mint sprigs (optional)

Pour a spoon of the crème de menthe into the bottom of 4 tall glasses. Add a little crushed ice and one quarter of the wine to each. Top up with Perrier water just before serving. Garnish with mint sprigs.
Calories per portion: 120 500 kJ

Citrus fizz

Metric	Imperial
170 g can frozen grape-fruit juice, thawed	6 oz can frozen grape-fruit juice, thawed
450 ml cold water	¾ pint cold water
Dash of bitters	Dash of bitters
241 ml bottle low-calorie bitter lemon	8½ fl oz bottle low-calorie bitter lemon
Ice	Ice
Lemon slices (optional)	Lemon slices (optional)

Combine the grapefruit juice, cold water and bitters in a jug and chill thoroughly. Just before serving carefully pour the bitter lemon down the side of the jug and stir gently with an up and down motion. Serve over ice and garnish each glass with a slice of lemon.
Calories per portion: 48 200 kJ

Orange and lemon cooler; Green summer cooler; Citrus fizz

Apricot-pineapple frost

Metric

½ kg can apricots
150 ml unsweetened
pineapple juice
½ teaspoon peppermint
essence
Crushed ice

To finish:
Mint sprigs

Imperial

1 lb can apricots
¼ pint unsweetened
pineapple juice
½ teaspoon peppermint
essence
Crushed ice

To finish:
Mint sprigs

Blend together the apricots, pineapple juice and peppermint essence in a liquidiser until frothy. Pour over crushed ice in tall glasses and garnish with mint sprigs.
Calories per portion: 78 300 kJ

Ginger-lime quencher

Metric

3 × 241 ml bottles low-
calorie dry ginger ale
230 ml low-calorie lime
juice cordial, undiluted
Ice cubes

To finish:
Fresh mint leaves

Imperial

3 × 8½ fl oz bottles low-
calorie dry ginger ale
8 fl oz low-calorie lime
juice cordial, undiluted
Ice cubes

To finish:
Fresh mint leaves

Combine the ginger ale with the lime cordial. Pour into four tall glasses, add the ice cubes, decorate with mint leaves and serve immediately.
Calories per portion: 16 80 kJ

Breakfast orange

Metric

300 ml fresh orange juice
4 × 15 ml spoons lemon
juice
2 drops liquid sweetener
(optional)
300 ml Perrier water

To finish:
2 × 15 ml spoons orange
rind, cut in thin strips

Imperial

½ pint fresh orange juice
4 tablespoons lemon
juice
2 drops liquid sweetener
(optional)
½ pint Perrier water

To finish:
2 tablespoons orange
rind, cut in thin strips

Mix together the fresh orange and lemon juice. Pour into four individual glasses. Add liquid sweetener if liked. Top up with chilled Perrier water and sprinkle with thin curls of orange rind.
Calories per portion: 70 300 kJ

Spicy iced coffee

Metric

450 ml skimmed milk
Liquid sweetener
2 × 15 ml spoons instant
coffee granules
½ teaspoon mixed spice
2 × 241 ml bottles low-
calorie ginger ale
Ice

Imperial

¾ pint skimmed milk
Liquid sweetener
2 tablespoons instant
coffee granules
½ teaspoon mixed spice
2 × 8½ fl oz bottles low-
calorie ginger ale
Ice

Blend together the skimmed milk, sweetener, coffee and mixed spice in a liquidiser until well mixed. Just before serving add the ginger ale. Serve over ice.
Calories per portion: 36 150 kJ

Ginger-lime quencher; Apricot-pineapple frost; Breakfast orange; Spicy iced coffee

Apple mint lamb

Metric	Imperial
1 small leg of lamb	*1 small leg of lamb*
1 × 15 ml spoon oil	*1 tablespoon oil*
4 × 15 ml spoons mint jelly	*4 tablespoons mint jelly*
225 g cooking apples, washed, cored, peeled and sliced	*8 oz cooking apples, washed, cored, peeled and sliced*
Salt and freshly ground black pepper	*Salt and freshly ground black pepper*
4 × 15 ml spoons finely chopped mint	*4 tablespoons finely chopped mint*

Cooking Time: 1½–2 hours
Oven: 190°C, 375°F, Gas Mark 5
Brush the lamb with the oil and cook in a moderate oven for 30 minutes per ½ kg (1 lb) or until a little pink juice flows. When almost cooked brush with the mint jelly, pour off the meat juices and cook the apple in this until soft. Beat well, season to taste and stir in chopped mint. Serve slices of lamb with minted apple sauce.
Calories per portion, allowing 100 g (4 oz) cooked lamb: 375 1,500 kJ

Vegetable sticks with come again dip

Metric	Imperial
100 g cottage cheese	*4 oz cottage cheese*
1 × 15 ml spoon Slimmer's French dressing (page 71)	*1 tablespoon Slimmer's French dressing (page 71)*
1 × 15 ml spoon finely chopped spring onion	*1 tablespoon finely chopped spring onion*
Salt and freshly ground black pepper	*Salt and freshly ground black pepper*
Few drops Worcestershire sauce	*Few drops Worcestershire sauce*
½ teaspoon lemon juice	*½ teaspoon lemon juice*
1 × 5 ml spoon fresh dill	*1 teaspoon fresh dill*

Mix all the ingredients together, blending well. Season to taste and chill for about 2 hours to allow flavours to blend. Serve as a dip for celery sticks, cucumber slices, green pepper sticks, radishes, carrot sticks and any other raw vegetable.
Calories per 15 ml spoon (1 tablespoon): 15 80 kJ

Funny face salad

Metric	Imperial
1 lettuce, washed	*1 lettuce, washed*
4 eggs, hard-boiled	*4 eggs, hard-boiled*
1 carrot, scrubbed	*1 carrot, scrubbed*
2 radishes, scrubbed	*2 radishes, scrubbed*
2 small gherkins	*2 small gherkins*
1 stick celery, scrubbed	*1 stick celery, scrubbed*

Shred the lettuce and use to line four individual plates. Halve the hard-boiled eggs and divide between the plates, cut side down. Garnish each egg with a piece of carrot, half a radish slice, pieces of gherkin and celery curls to represent nose, mouth, eyes and hair of funny face. Serve with main dish or as an appetiser.
Calories per portion: 90 350 kJ

Fruit kebabs

Metric	Imperial
1 green apple	*1 green apple*
1 red apple	*1 red apple*
2 bananas	*2 bananas*
Lemon juice	*Lemon juice*
2 large oranges	*2 large oranges*
12 black grapes	*12 black grapes*
50 g Edam cheese, cubed	*2 oz Edam cheese, cubed*
Mint sprigs (optional)	*Mint sprigs (optional)*

Cooking Time: 5 minutes

Wash, core and thickly slice the apples. Peel and thickly slice the bananas. Brush the apple and banana slices with a little lemon juice to prevent discolouring. Remove all peel and pith from the oranges and segment. Thread the apples, bananas, oranges, grapes and cheese alternately on four skewers. Cook under a prepared high grill until heated through. If cooking over charcoal, throw a few sprigs of mint on the coals during cooking to give the fruit a minted flavour.
Calories per portion: 97 400 kJ

Vegetable sticks with come again dip; Apple mint lamb; Funny face salad; Fruit kebabs

Chilled chocolate soufflé

Metric	Imperial
450 ml skimmed milk	¾ pint skimmed milk
2 × 15 ml spoons cornflour	2 tablespoons cornflour
2 × 15 ml spoons cocoa powder	2 tablespoons cocoa powder
8 drops liquid sweetener	8 drops liquid sweetener
4 × 15 ml spoons skimmed milk	4 tablespoons skimmed milk
4 egg whites	4 egg whites
¼ teaspoon vanilla essence	¼ teaspoon vanilla essence
4 × 15 ml spoons double cream	4 tablespoons double cream
15 g plain chocolate, grated	½ oz plain chocolate, grated

Cooking Time: about 10 minutes

Prepare 4 small soufflé dishes by tying a double piece of lightly-oiled greaseproof paper around them, extending 5 cm (2 in) above the top. Scald the skimmed milk. Mix the cornflour, cocoa and sweetener with the cold skimmed milk to form a smooth paste. Slowly add to the hot skimmed milk and cook gently until the mixture thickens, stirring constantly. Remove from the heat and cool slightly. Whip 3 of the egg whites with the vanilla essence until stiff and fold into the cooled chocolate mixture. Carefully spoon into the prepared soufflé dishes. Chill thoroughly. When cool remove the greaseproof bands. Whisk the remaining egg white until stiff and fold in the lightly-whipped double cream. Pipe in swirls on top of the soufflés and decorate with the grated chocolate.
Calories per portion: 180 700 kJ

Iceberg meringues with strawberry filling

Metric	Imperial
3 large egg whites	3 large egg whites
1 × 5 ml spoon cream of tartar	1 teaspoon cream of tartar
3 × 15 ml spoons dry skimmed milk	3 tablespoons dry skimmed milk
6 saccharin tablets	6 saccharin tablets
1 small egg white	1 small egg white
4 × 15 ml spoons double cream	4 tablespoons double cream
1 × 5 ml spoon vanilla essence	1 teaspoon vanilla essence
225 g strawberries	8 oz strawberries

Cooking Time: 30 minutes
Oven: 150°C, 300°F, Gas Mark 2

Whisk the egg whites lightly, sprinkle in the cream of tartar and continue until the mixture forms peaks. Add the skimmed milk and 6 crushed saccharin tablets, a tablespoon at a time, until the peaks are stiff. Pipe on to non-stick paper on a baking sheet. Cook in a cool oven for about 20–30 minutes. Cool and lift off paper. Meanwhile whisk the small egg white until stiff, fold in the whipped cream, vanilla essence and the washed, hulled and sliced strawberries. Sandwich the meringues together with the strawberry filling.
Calories per portion: 182 700 kJ

Baked rice custards

Metric	Imperial
450 ml skimmed milk	¾ pint skimmed milk
1 vanilla pod	1 vanilla pod
2 large eggs	2 large eggs
Pinch of salt	Pinch of salt
150 g cooked round-grain rice	5 oz cooked round-grain rice
Liquid sweetener	Liquid sweetener
To finish:	To finish:
1 small orange, sliced	1 small orange, sliced

Cooking Time: 50 minutes
Oven: 160°C, 325°F, Gas Mark 3

Pour the milk into a saucepan, add the vanilla pod and bring slowly to the boil. Leave to infuse for about 10 minutes. Crack the eggs into a deep bowl and whisk with the salt until well blended and pale in colour. Remove the vanilla pod from the milk, rinse and dry for further use. Pour the milk on to the eggs, stirring, and strain into a measuring jug. Add the cooked rice and sweetener to taste, blending thoroughly. Divide the custard mixture between 4 dariole moulds or ramekin dishes of 150 ml (¼ pint) capacity. Place in a large roasting tin in 1.5 cm (½ in) cold water. Cover with a double sheet of kitchen foil and cook in the centre of a slow oven for 45–50 minutes, or until firm in the centre. Serve hot or cold with a twist of orange.
Calories per portion: 150 600 kJ

Baked rice custards; Iceberg meringues; Chilled chocolate soufflé; Foamy baked apples

Foamy baked apples

Metric

4 large dessert apples
1 egg
Juice of 2 oranges or
150 ml
6 drops liquid sweetener

To finish:
Orange slices

Imperial

4 large dessert apples
1 egg
Juice of 2 oranges or
¼ pint
6 drops liquid sweetener

To finish:
Orange slices

Cooking Time: 40 minutes
Oven: 190°C, 375°F, Gas Mark 5

Wash and core the apples and wrap in foil or in a roasting bag (pierced). Place in a roasting tin and bake for about 40 minutes until cooked. Meanwhile place the egg and orange juice in a basin over a pan of hot water. Whisk for about 10 minutes until foamy and slightly thickened. Sweeten to taste with the sweetener. Serve on top of the baked apples, garnished with the orange slices.
Calories per portion: 95 400 kJ

Crispy fingers; Sausage propellers

Crispy fingers

Metric	Imperial
4 slices low-calorie bread	4 slices low-calorie bread
12 canned sardines	12 canned sardines
1 × 15 ml spoon tomato ketchup	1 tablespoon tomato ketchup
Salt and freshly ground black pepper	Salt and freshly ground black pepper
4 egg whites	4 egg whites
50 g Edam cheese, grated	2 oz Edam cheese, grated

Cooking Time: 15 minutes
Oven: 150°C, 300°F, Gas Mark 2

Toast the bread lightly. Remove crusts and cut into fingers. Drain and flake the sardines and mix with the tomato ketchup and seasoning to taste. Spread equal amounts of the mixture on the toasted fingers. Beat the egg whites until stiff, fold in the grated cheese and pile on top of the sardine fingers. Bake in a cool oven for about 15 minutes or until the egg white is nicely browned. Serve hot.
Calories per portion: 205 800 kJ

Sausage propellers

Metric	Imperial
8 small sausages	8 small sausages
8 lean rashers bacon	8 lean rashers bacon
25 g Edam cheese, cubed	1 oz Edam cheese, cubed
Apple and cabbage slaw (page 68)	Apple and cabbage slaw (page 68)

Cooking Time: 10 minutes

Wrap each sausage in a rasher of bacon and cook under a hot grill for 5–10 minutes until crisp and brown. Remove and thread two sausages, with the bacon, on to each of four cocktail sticks to form propellers. Finish with a cube of cheese. Serve on a bed of Apple and cabbage slaw.
Calories per portion: 370 1,500 kJ

92

Saucy pinwheels; Meat loaf

Saucy pinwheels

Metric

1 × 15 ml spoon oil
2 × 15 ml spoons finely grated onion
2 × 15 ml spoons low-calorie breadcrumbs
2 × 5 ml spoons finely chopped fresh herbs
Salt and freshly ground pepper
550 g plaice fillets
2 × 15 ml spoons lemon juice
350 ml water
1 × 15 ml spoon cornflour

Imperial

1 tablespoon oil
2 tablespoons finely grated onion
2 tablespoons low-calorie breadcrumbs
2 teaspoons finely chopped fresh herbs
Salt and freshly ground pepper
1¼ lb plaice fillets
2 tablespoons lemon juice
12 fl oz water
1 tablespoon cornflour

Cooking Time: 40 minutes
Oven: 160°C, 325°F, Gas Mark 3

Heat the oil and use to sauté the onion until soft but not brown. Stir in the breadcrumbs, herbs and seasoning to taste. Turn the fish fillets in this mixture and roll up. Place in a baking dish. Mix the lemon juice with the water and a little salt and pour over the fish. Bake in a moderate oven for about 30 minutes. Place the pinwheels on a hot serving dish and keep warm. Moisten the cornflour with a little water, stir into the fish juices and cook until smooth. Taste and adjust seasoning; pour over fish.
Calories per portion: 145 600 kJ

Meat Loaf

Metric

350 g lean minced beef
1 small onion, peeled and chopped
1 × 15 ml spoon ketchup
½ teaspoon salt
Freshly ground black pepper
1 × 15 ml spoon Worcestershire sauce
Pinch grated nutmeg
Pinch ground allspice
Pinch dried thyme
1 × 5 ml spoon finely chopped parsley
1 large egg
2 eggs, hard-boiled

Imperial

12 oz lean minced beef
1 small onion, peeled and chopped
1 tablespoon ketchup
½ teaspoon salt
Freshly ground black pepper
1 tablespoon Worcestershire sauce
Pinch grated nutmeg
Pinch ground allspice
Pinch dried thyme
1 teaspoon finely chopped parsley
1 large egg
2 eggs, hard-boiled

Cooking Time: 45–60 minutes
Oven: 180°C, 350°F, Gas Mark 4

Mix all the ingredients together, except for the hard-boiled eggs. Shape into a flat rectangle and place the hard-boiled eggs down the centre. Roll the meat mixture around the eggs, using the fingers, and place in a small loaf tin. Cover with foil and bake in a moderate oven for 45–60 minutes. Remove foil and cook for a further 10 minutes to brown the top. Serve in slices, hot or cold, with a crisp salad.
Calories per portion: 275 1,100 kJ

Food value table

Food	Portion	Calories	Kilojoules (kJ)	Food	Portion	Calories	Kilojoules (kJ)
Anchovies	25g/1oz (6 fillets)	40	150	Cornflour	25g/1oz	100	450
Apples	25g/1oz	10	50	Courgettes	25g/1oz	2	10
	1 medium (100g/4oz)	40	150	Crab meat, boiled	25g/1oz	35	150
Apricots, fresh	25g/1oz (1 medium)	5	20	Cream, double	2 × 15ml spoons = 25g/1oz	130	550
canned	25g/1oz (1 medium)	30	150				
dried	25g/1oz	50	200	single	2 × 15ml spoons = 25g/1oz	60	250
Artichokes, Globe	25g/1oz	5	20				
Jerusalem	25g/1oz	5	20	soured	2 × 15ml spoons = 25g/1oz	55	200
Asparagus	25g/1oz	5	20				
Aubergines	25g/1oz	5	20	Cucumber	25g/1oz	3	10
Avocado Pear	25g/1oz	25	100	Currants	25g/1oz	70	300
	1 medium (300g/10oz)	250	1,050	Damsons, raw	25g/1oz	10	50
Bacon, lean, raw	25g/1oz	115	500	Duck, meat only, raw	25g/1oz	70	300
gammon, raw	25g/1oz	90	400	Eggs, whole	1 small	70	300
Bananas	25g/1oz	15	50		1 standard	80	350
	1 medium (100g/4oz)	60	250		1 large	90	400
Bass, steamed	25g/1oz	20	80	whole	25g/1oz	45	200
Beans, baked	25g/1oz	25	100	white	25g/1oz	10	50
broad	25g/1oz	10	50	yolk	25g/1oz	100	450
butter	25g/1oz	75	300	Flour	25g/1oz	100	450
haricot	25g/1oz	75	300	Garlic	1 clove	2	10
runner	25g/1oz	5	20	Gelatine powder	8 × 5ml spoons = 25g/1oz	100	450
Beef, very lean	25g/1oz	75	300				
Beetroot, raw	25g/1oz	10	50	Gooseberries, raw	25g/1oz	10	45
Blackberries	25g/1oz	10	50	Grapefruit, flesh	25g/1oz	5	20
Blackcurrants	25g/1oz	10	50	whole	1 medium (100g/4oz)	30	150
Bread, white or brown	25g/1oz	70	300	Grapes	25g/1oz	15	60
average slice large loaf		80	350	Haddock, white, raw	25g/1oz	20	90
average slice small loaf		50	200	smoked, raw	25g/1oz	20	90
Broccoli	25g/1oz	5	20	Hake, fillets only, raw	25g/1oz	25	100
Brussel Sprouts	25g/1oz	10	50	Halibut, raw	25g/1oz	30	150
Butter	25g/1oz	225	950	Ham, York, raw	25g/1oz	145	600
Buttermilk	600ml/1 pint	235	1,000	lean only, boiled	25g/1oz	60	250
Cabbage, red or white	25g/1oz	5	20	Herring, raw	25g/1oz	65	280
Carrots	25g/1oz	5	20	Honey	25g/1oz	80	350
Cauliflower	25g/1oz	5	20	Ice cream	25g/1oz	55	250
Celery	25g/1oz	3	10	Jam	25g/1oz	75	300
Cheese, Austrian smoked	25g/1oz	80	350	Jelly, made up	600ml/1 pint	420	1,800
Camembert	25g/1oz	90	400	cubes	25g/1oz	75	300
Cheddar	25g/1oz	120	500	Kidneys, raw	25g/1oz	30–35	150
Cheshire	25g/1oz	110	450	Kippers, raw	25g/1oz	30	150
Cottage	25g/1oz	30	150	Lamb, very lean only, raw	25g/1oz	75	300
Cream	25g/1oz	230	950	Lard	25g/1oz	260	1,100
Curd	25g/1oz	40	150	Leeks, raw	25g/1oz	10	50
Danish Blue	25g/1oz	105	450	Lemon, raw	25g/1oz	5	20
Edam	25g/1oz	90	400	Lemon juice	2 × 15ml spoons	2	10
Gouda	25g/1oz	95	400	Lentils, raw	25g/1oz	85	350
Gruyère	25g/1oz	130	550	Lettuce, raw	25g/1oz	3	10
Leicester	25g/1oz	110	450	Liver, raw	25g/1oz	40–45	150–200
Parmesan	25g/1oz	120	500	Macaroni, raw	25g/1oz	100	400
Stilton	25g/1oz	135	600	boiled	25g/1oz	30	150
Wensleydale	25g/1oz	115	500	Mackerel, raw	25g/1oz	30	150
Cherries, fresh	25g/1oz	10	50	Margarine	25g/1oz	225	1,000
glacé	25g/1oz	60	250	Marmalade	25g/1oz	75	300
Chicken, flesh only, raw	25g/1oz	35	150	Marrow, boiled	25g/1oz	2	10
Chives, raw	25g/1oz	10	50	Melon	25g/1oz	5	20
Chocolate, milk	25g/1oz	165	700	Milk, whole	600ml/1 pint	380	1,600
plain	25g/1oz	155	650	skimmed	600ml/1 pint	190	800
Cod, raw	25g/1oz	20	90	Mushrooms, raw	25g/1oz	2	10
Cod's roe, raw	25g/1oz	35	150				
Cornflakes and most cereals	25g/1oz	105	450				

Food	Portion	Calories	Kilojoules (kJ)
Mustard, made up	25g/1oz	10	50
dry	25g/1oz	130	500
Nuts, Almonds, shelled	25g/1oz	170	750
Brazils, shelled	25g/1oz	180	800
Chestnuts, shelled	25g/1oz	50	200
Peanuts, shelled	25g/1oz	170	750
Peanuts, roast & salted	25g/1oz	180	800
Walnuts, shelled	25g/1oz	155	650
Oil, olive or corn	30ml/1 fl. oz	265	1,100
Olives	25g/1oz (8–10)	25	100
Onions, raw	25g/1oz	5	20
Oranges	25g/1oz	10	50
	1 medium	40	150
Parsnips, raw	25g/1oz	5	20
Peaches, raw	25g/1oz	10	50
	1 medium (100g/4oz)	40	150
Pears, raw	25g/1oz	10	50
	1 medium (100g/4oz)	40	150
Peas, fresh or frozen	25g/1oz	20	90
canned	25g/1oz	25	100
Peppers, red or green	25g/1oz	10	50
Pineapple, fresh	25g/1oz	15	60
canned	25g/1oz	20	90
Plaice, raw	25g/1oz	15	60
Plums, raw	25g/1oz	10	50
Pork, very lean only	25g/1oz	35	150
Potatoes, raw	25g/1oz	25	100
Prawns, whole, raw	25g/1oz	10	50
flesh only	25g/1oz	30	150
Rabbit, meat only, raw	25g/1oz	50	200
Radishes, raw	25g/1oz	5	20
Raspberries, raw	25g/1oz	5	20
Redcurrants, raw	25g/1oz	5	20
Rhubarb, raw	25g/1oz	2	10
Rice, raw	25g/1oz	100	450
boiled	25g/1oz	35	150
Salmon, fresh, raw	25g/1oz	55	250
canned	25g/1oz	40	150
Sardines, canned	25g/1oz	85	350
Sausage, average, raw	25g/1oz	100	400
Sole, raw	25g/1oz	15	60
Soup, consommé	300ml/½ pint	40–65	150–250
thin eg chicken noodle	300ml/½ pint	65–100	300–400
thick	300ml/½ pint	90–200	400–800
Spaghetti, raw	25g/1oz	105	400
boiled	25g/1oz	35	150
Spinach	25g/1oz	5	20
Spring Greens	25g/1oz	3	10
Stock cube	each	15	60
Strawberries	25g/1oz	5	20
Suet	25g/1oz	260	1,100
Sugar, white or brown	25g/1oz	110	500
Swedes, raw	25g/1oz	5	20
Sweetcorn, canned or frozen	25g/1oz	25	100
Syrup	25g/1oz	85	350
Tangerines	25g/1oz	5	20
Tomatoes, raw	25g/1oz	5	20
	1 medium (50g/2oz)	10	50
Tomato purée	25g/1oz	40	150

Food	Portion	Calories	Kilojoules (kJ)
Tongue	25g/1oz	85	350
Trout, raw	25g/1oz	25	100
Tuna, canned in oil	25g/1oz	75	300
Turkey, meat only, raw	25g/1oz	35	150
Turnips, raw	25g/1oz	5	20
Veal, fillet, raw	25g/1oz	30	150
Vinegar	30ml/1 fl. oz.	1	5
Watercress	25g/1oz	5	20
Whiting, raw	25g/1oz	15	60
Yogurt, plain low-fat	30ml/1 fl. oz.	15	50
	142g/5oz carton	75	300
fruit flavoured	142g/5oz carton	125	500

Drink	Quantity	Calories	Kilojoules (kJ)
Bacardi	1 measure	63	250
Beer, draught bitter	600ml/1 pint	180	800
draught mild	600ml/1 pint	140	600
pale ale	600ml/1 pint	180	800
lager	600ml/1 pint	150	600
brown ale	600ml/1 pint	160	650
bottle stout	600ml/1 pint	200	800
Brandy	liqueur glass	75	300
Bourbon	liqueur glass	65	280
Campari	1 measure	120	500
Cider, dry	600ml/1 pint	200	800
sweet	600ml/1 pint	240	1,000
Cocktails	Vary according to ingredients	115–300	500–1,000
Gin	1 measure	55	200
Liqueurs	Vary according to type	65–90	300–400
Port	1 measure	75	300
Rum	1 measure	75	300
Sherry, dry	1 measure	55	200
sweet	1 measure	65	280
Vermouth, dry	1 measure	55	200
sweet	1 measure	75	300
Vodka	1 measure	65	280
Whisky	1 measure	60	250
Wine, dry	150ml/¼ pint	90	400
sweet	150ml/¼ pint	115	500

Soft Drinks

Drink	Quantity	Calories	Kilojoules (kJ)
Apple juice, unsweetened	small glass	50	200
Blackcurrant concentrate	1 × 15ml (tablespoon)	35	150
Grapefruit juice, unsweetened	small glass	55	200
Lemonade	600ml/1 pint	120	500
Orange juice, unsweetened	small glass	60	250
Tomato juice	small glass	25	100
Low-calorie minerals		0	0
Low-calorie orange squash	per oz	5	20
Low-calorie Lemon squash	per oz	2	10

Index